WEITCHIE

Spirit of the Redwoods

by David Coe

Q.E.D. Press

Fort Bragg, California

This is a work of fiction. Any resemblance between the characters depicted in this novel and real persons, living or dead, is purely coincidental.

Cover photograph by Sean Sprague
Cover design by Chuck Hathaway, Mendocino Graphics

Published by Q.E.D. Press
155 Cypress Street
Fort Bragg, CA 95437
(707) 964-9520

First Edition

Printed on recycled paper.
Manufactured in the U.S.A.

ISBN No. 0-936609-20-6

Dedication

To the patient teachers of the College of the Siskiyous English Department: Jim, Ernie, Michael and, especially, Caroline. And to Jim W., who taught me there cannot be drama without conflict. Just the way we are.

The impotent speak of her scars

saying, note the clan membership,
the initiation into secret practices.

Pimps hawk her green virtues
in the city streets.

The grove's last rings
unfurl among serpents.

If the mycelial net unravels
not even the ground will break her fall

—*Cynthia Frank*

WEITCHIE

(Wee-et-chia)

Spirit of the Redwoods

PRELUDE

Hard to believe how things can change so fast in a man's life. Lost my job, the place where I lived, and, most important, the way I thought about things. I made a big mistake last fall, didn't mean to, but it happened. Now Weitchie's gone. I have to deal with that, and writing everything down helps get it all straight in my mind.

Dropped out of school early, but I always liked words and reading—books, magazines, anything took my eye. Read some fantasy too, even some New Age stuff, but I never believed any of it. Not until I met Weitchie. Not sure anymore what else is real, but she was. And I am, now.

Meeting her changed my ideas about trees, too. When I worked for a road-grading contractor, trees were just more logs for cutting and dragging out to a mill, but there must have been something different in my heart, otherwise why live and work around the forest? I could have gone to the city like so many others, but for all my thirty-six years my life has been the forest. Fought fires, sprayed brush, did grunt labor and ran around for logging contractors for eighteen years. Just a go-fer. No complaints, but everything is changed now. After meeting Weitchie, I made another job for myself. A job that gives me a lot of time for thinking and writing.

It's spring now, and I'd like to tell you about what happened late last summer and fall. How we all met Weitchie in her small grove of ancient redwood trees and what happened there. Saw some of it myself, talked with Michael and Frank, heard their side, and when I met Maude again last winter, she told me the rest. Maude has a real good memory, which I guess goes with being educated, and people sometimes like telling me things they wouldn't feel good about telling others. Been that way all my life. Maybe it goes with being a quiet sort, 'cause I never liked getting caught up in other people's stuff, getting involved. Used to be mostly content just watching and listening.

I'm not like that anymore, and if they're not already looking for me, they will be when they read this. So just call me Joe. It's not the name I was born with, but it'll do for now, and I'll explain the rest after you've read my story.

I always liked driving along that part of the coast highway that winds through the Redwood National Park like a narrow river of black through a green and brown cathedral of ancient redwood trees. You've seen that stretch of highway, or pictures of it, real nice, very different from the land just off the highway past the park. There's an old logging road there, running east. It probably wouldn't even be noticed by most people. Just a rough strip of dusty brown funneling off from the smooth black asphalt and turning quickly as it cuts through the thin fringe of the thousand year old trees they left along the highway as a visual buffer for the tourists.

I want to tell what happened as it happened, chronologically, as Maude would say, so while this story's not about hippies, they sort of started everything. I'll begin with Maude, her partner Jeb, and the troop of hippies that arrived at a dusty old campsite on a slope near the end of that logging road. The whole area had been logged some years before and the slope was dotted with scattered brush, clumps of grass and weeds, and rotting stumps.

1

THE SCENE.

...I remember the day it all started, because it was a real warm day, the sort we don't often get here on the coast in the summer. It was Sunday, August 6, and a few thin clouds were drifting in off the ocean, laying a veil over the lowering sun. Maude and the others had just come from celebrating a pagan holiday up north, something they called Lughnasadh. Never did find out what that meant. It was late in the day as Jeb drove Maude's new van off the road, parking beside a blackened, stone-ringed firepit that lay between a small chuckling brook and a large rotting stump.

Jeb was a lanky, graying, pony-tailed man, and he most always wore a cowboy hat. As he stepped out and stood looking back down the road, the bright forest scene painted on the sides of the van in blues, browns, and greens, wavered and danced in the lifting cloud of fine dust. Behind the van was an old delivery truck painted purple and a school bus with a wooden upper story built onto it. The bus was painted orange and green. I saw them myself a few days later. They sure looked odd.

Two dented, colorless Volkswagen bugs pulled up behind the bus, and as they stopped, a pair of black crows lifted heavily from the ground beyond the brook. The crows complained to each other the way they most always do as they flapped heavily toward the near ridge to the east. "Crawk, craw, craw, crawk".

Finally, as Jeb waited, a black motorcycle rolled up, sputtered and died. The young rider kicked the stand in place and got off, hanging his helmet on the handlebar and looking up at the older man...

"Hi Jeb, sorry I kinda got behind. There was a elk on the road an' he ran back and forth all over. I had to swerve like crazy 'fore I finally hit him."

"Elk? You hit an elk, Hensley?"

"Yeah, honest. They got some down at that park, like big squirrels with horns. Don't think I hurt him any, he ran off in all directions. Wasn't limpin' or nothin'. Didn't hurt the bike neither."

"He ran off in all directions?" As Jeb shook his head, staring at the younger man, the bike rider nodded and turned to join the others as they piled out of the vehicles with surprising numbers of children among them. The young people, dressed mostly in t-shirts, faded jeans or granny dresses, stayed close, looking about and talking quietly.

Jeb walked around the van as Maude slid out the other side. "This the place, Maude? Same place we camped last spring?"

Her eyes met his, thin lips lighting with a secret smile as she reached behind the seat for a slender wand of polished white wood and then closed the door. "Yes, this is the place, still the same strong feeling of nature, just as I remember. As though untouched forest were still here on this slope, unseen. And not just the ghosts of trees such as Clare often reports seeing, a feeling of living forest. A curious sensation. This place has more of a feeling of undiluted nature than even the groves in the park. I do not understand why that should be, but this time we have Clare, the troop, and the ritual we have rehearsed with them, and today's horoscope is much more positive than the one last spring. Very powerful. This time we will solve the mystery and discover just why this particular location feels so different from others like it."

Maude stepped away from the van, stretching on tiptoe, braceleted arms overhead, strong face tilted upward. Relaxing, she stepped to the half-rotted stump and laid a hand on the rough bark, looking toward the setting sun. "A sorry day it will be when all the ancient forests are gone. There is so much we might learn from the natural world if some of it could be left untouched. So much will be lost." She turned back to Jeb, almost as tall as he, and laid a hand on his arm, smiling. "While everyone is quiet and waiting I will do a short ritual, then we can make camp."

With the wand held high in both hands, Maude, slender with long, graying braids, stepped to a flat spot beside the brook. Closing her eyes, she began a soft wordless chant. As the sounds grew stronger, she spun about, the ankle-length white skirt swinging around her legs. Stopping, facing the barren hillside above the slope, the wand came slowly down, pointing toward a clump of bushes growing between two outcrops of crumbling, gray rock.

As the chant faded and she opened her eyes, everything lay still until a bluejay squawked a query from a small, stunted sapling on the hillside and flew up a narrow ravine behind the bushes. Maude looked after the jay, smiling, then turned, looking up at Jeb, standing just above her, stroking his bearded chin. "Something there, Maude?"

"Yes, where the brook flows out from under the

Gaultheria bushes, between those two outcrops of rock. It feels as though something is there."

"You mean that clump of salal there? Didn't hardly notice it last time we was here. Looks to be just a skinny, rocky ravine there behind 'em. Don't look inviting. Shall I call Clare? Want to put her in trance and let her look? Or maybe later when the moon's up, we can do the ceremony."

"Truly fascinating. I have never felt such a pull from the wand before. I do not understand this at all."

The motorcycle rider, all elbows and knees with fair hair swinging about skinny shoulders, came up and stood beside them, staring in the same direction. "What you see on the hillside there, Maude?"

"Do you see anything, Hensley?"

"Just brush an' rock, nothin' much. That a buzzard way up there? That little dot. Looks like he's buzzin' right along on the breeze. Think he might come down an' buzz us?"

Maude glanced up. "A Cathartidae, North American vulture. Be serious, Hensley. Look at the narrow ravine and the brook."

"Well, sure, Maude."

"Where does it come from, that brook, before it flows under the bushes?"

"Guess there's a spring behind this here clump of bush. What else?"

"I believe we will see what else...later."

"Right on, Maude, you'll show us somethin', know you will. Always do." Hensley turned, grinning at Jed. "Camp here? Ugly with all the dead stumps an' broken cans an' junk layin' around, but there's plenty of good water. Dusty, no shade, but we got everythin' we'll need to hang out. What ya say, Maude?"

"Wait a few minutes more, Hensley, and no cannabis or anything. Just wait."

"Aw, Maude, like you said, we didn't bring nothin'. Not this time, though I, well..." Hensley shrugged and turned, walking back to the group by the bus, talking with them quietly.

"What you think, Maude?"

"We will see. We must not hurry or take a chance that we might spoil our seeking. We need time to attune ourselves to the unique energy of this place. This evening we will complete our preparation, tomorrow we will do the ceremony. The exact time of the full moon falls tomorrow afternoon, so the ceremony can be done either day."

Jeb nodded, scratching an ear. "Camp now?" She nodded and he turned, waving at the others as he walked toward the bus, indicating with gestures where the camp would be set. "Tom, latrine down there below the road."

A stocky, dark, wild-haired younger man nodded and walked down the slope in the golden sunset with a spade and two toilet seats on a wooden box.

I guess they had camped together enough they mostly knew what to do. Maude told me all of this later, after we got acquainted.

The next day, the last of the California sunset was fading into dusky rose and darkness as the half-naked children chased shrieking about the campsite and the adults finished their meal, sitting on stools or sleeping pads on the ground around the campfire, eating from wooden bowls with chopsticks. Like glowing flower petals, the flames in the stone-ringed firepit lit the scene with a flickering light, making the painted sides of the vehicles jiggle and dance. As the disk of the moon rose through the tree tops on the ridge to the east, Maude, sitting on a campstool, whistled softly and the group quieted.

Facing the moon, bracelets and rings glinting in the firelight, Maude raised her arms, beginning a sing-song chant. The others laid aside their bowls and, straightening, joined her, women's voices rising above hers, tones of the men below. The children quickly nestled in among the adults and, eyes shining, joined in with uncertain treble voices.

The chant faded into the silence of the open space and the group got comfortable as Maude began a story. "A long time ago there was a land far from here called Greece. The people there were very different from us. They did not have television, cars, or jet planes, and were just beginning to read and write and wonder about the world around them. Most lived in tents or crude huts, with campfires, and no one had water in their houses, toilets, or electric lights."

"How'd they get anywhere or know what's happening?" The sleepy-eyed girl pushed away from her mother, looking up at Maude.

"They did not, Star. Most people did not travel, or know what was happening more than a day's walk away, unless a trader came by and told them, but the traders did not usually go very far either. Anyway, a big difference between those people and ourselves was in religion. Today people think of Spirit as all in One Being they call God. In those past times, people saw Spirit in all things: in all green, living things, in animals, rocks, rivers, mountains, everything. And they thought there were special places, places where there was more Spirit than other places." She paused, pulling a fringed shawl about her shoulders as a breath of wind stirred the dancing flames.

"They woulda liked the redwoods, I bet!"

"Yes, Joey, I believe they would have liked the redwoods very much. That is partly why we are here."

"But no trees here. They cut 'em all away. All gone."

"That is true, Star. They took away all the redwood trees, but there is Spirit here, nearby. I can feel it. We will see tomorrow whether the spirit of the trees is still here.

The long ago Greeks would have thought this a very magical place. Very magical. And for them Magic and Spirit were much the same, and they were right." Maude raised her head, staring at the moon.

"I will tell you a story about one young Greek, one who did not believe what his parents and teachers told him. He thought all the talk about Spirit in everything was silly. He would tell everyone, 'I've never seen anything in the woods but trees and animals. I've never seen anything in the water but rocks and fish. I only believe what I see.' His elders just shook their heads and left him alone. They could see there was no use telling him anything."

"Like Hensley?"

"Shh. One day as this young man was setting traps for small animals in the woods, he stopped for a rest, sitting with his back against a great tree on the top of a low, rocky hill. 'Phooey,' he thought. 'Why should I spend all my time setting snares and helping my father with his dumb olive trees. There must be something better in the world, and I'm going to find it.' Thinking like that, he fell asleep. And in his sleep he dreamt that he returned home, packed a few things and, saying goodbye to his parents and sisters, started down the narrow dirt path that led toward the nearest city."

Jeb added more sticks to the fire. It crackled, sinking, and a lone coyote barked in the distance, then howled once. Maude pulled the shawl tighter.

"After the young man, in his dream, had left the village clearing and entered the woods, a strange thing happened. He kept walking but didn't move past one large, spreading tree. Half afraid, he ran. It made no difference. The big tree stayed right beside him. Nothing changed. Out of breath, he stopped, and as he stared wildly about, a beautiful, red-haired young woman stepped out of the tree smiling at him, beckoning him to..."

"Umm...lovely, sad night." A high, thin voice interrupted Maude's tale. "Lovely sad people in the moon's soft light. Sad, dying trees. Death, so much of death. Trees all cut, gone, stumps bleeding, rotting, dying. Life flown all away. Sad, sad. Power all gone. Only sad dying stumps, rocks, weeds, ugly black crows flapping and...wait! Oh wait! There! There!" The slender, colorless young woman turned, rising awkwardly to her knees, one long, slender arm pointing toward the barren hillside. Moonlight reflected from two glass beads in the headband above her closed eyes and expressionless face.

"There, Maude, everybody, there! Life! Oh, so beautiful. Trees, flowers, happy birds singing...oh, hear the birds, Maude! Hear the birds so sweet they sing. In the night, the smell of flowers like honey and birds singing. And the great owl...oh, life is there! And power!"

Maude leaned forward. "Where, Clare. What do you see?"

Jeb stirred the fire, adding more sticks and half rotted wood. "Never acted like this before." He spoke softly, as if to himself. Others about the fire murmured, looking at each other or staring open mouthed at Clare.

"There, Maude. Tall, green trees, birds, life! All there in the wonderful, magic canyon. Right there! So beautiful, so full of life. There, behind those bushes, Maude." Clare stood, eyes still closed, facing up the slope, one arm pointing. "Can't you see? Right behind those tall bushes, those rocks. Where the little brook runs so merrily, the blessed, happy water with little frogs and fishes swimming in it runs out of the canyon so full of life. The forest life is not all gone, it's there in the canyon. Hiding."

"You are seeing a canyon full of birds and redwood trees? Hiding?"

"Oh yes, so full of tall trees and full of life, and

sleeping power." A sly smile curved her lips. "But only I can see the beautiful tall trees and I want to go there. I want to touch the sleeping power."

As she slowly stepped forward, Hensley jumped up, moving out of her way, face troubled. "Clare, you're asleep again, where you goin', what're you..."

Maude moved quickly, stepping over the staring children, her shawl slipping to the ground unnoticed. Taking hold of Clare's arm, her moon-shadow covering the smaller, slender form, Maude asked, "Clare, where are you going? Do you really see trees in a canyon there beyond those rocks in that hillside?"

"Oh yes, Maude. Magic trees, hiding from the loggers. But only I can see them. I want to touch the trees, Maude, want to touch the great trees that fill the canyon like bright stars fill the sky. Want to touch their light and feel their sleeping power. Yes, oh yes, I want to touch the beautiful trees and the power." Clare tugged at Maude's hold.

"But, Clare, you..."

"Come, Maude, come everybody. Come with me to the beautiful magic canyon. Come, I can show you the way."

"You can lead us there?"

"Yes, I can lead you, only I. The trees hide from the loggers and their machines. Hide from everybody, but I see them. Come, Maude, if you dare."

Maude hesitated, then took Clare's hand and held out her other hand to Hensley. "Cathy, Hank, stay with the children. The rest, come, hold hands."

One by one the group, ten of them, moved around the fire, joining hands, the last wrapping her fingers about Jeb's broad palm as the awed children watched. Maude nodded, eyes bright in the moonlight. "Lead us then, Clare."

"Yes, I will lead you. Through the bushes where the

brook runs so sweetly with little frogs and fishes singing. I will lead you through the entrance to the magic canyon." Murmuring, the group started up the slope beside the brook.

Jeb whispered in his deep voice, "Is a sort of haze there in the moonlight, Maude. Up that ravine behind the bushes. Yeah, maybe something is there."

"We will see. Lead us, Clare, to your magic trees in a magic canyon."

"Yes, but you don't believe so it won't be there if you look. You don't believe anything, Maude, not truly. Everybody close your eyes. Trust me."

"Yes, Clare, we will close our eyes. We trust you."

"And be real quiet. We mustn't disturb the Presence, she might not like us if we bother her. Real quiet. And everybody take off your shoes. I lead you through water, to sacred ground."

With Jeb last in line, they hastily took off their shoes and, linking hands again, followed Clare into the brook, pushing through the clump of salal between the two rock outcrops. Jeb swore as he slipped on a moss-clothed rock, falling to his knees in the cold water of the brook. "Damn!"

"Shh!"

"Stubbed mah toe."

"Shh."

The group worked their way up the narrow ravine, feeling for footing on the smooth, mossy rocks, until they turned a corner around another outcrop of the gray rock that stood out from the side of the ravine.

Clare stopped and the others crowded around. "Now, open your eyes," she whispered, soft voice triumphant. "Open your eyes and look, my sad friends. Look! Smell the honey-sweet flowers. Hear the sweet little owl call her mate through the great trees. And the great owl waits in the tall trees, watching."

Members of the group half-turned, looking about, murmuring. Some leaned back, trying to see the tops of the trees. "My God, it's real!" Jeb shook his head. "Just around this corner of rock. Ravine opens into a whole natural redwood grove. But no birds singing."

Clare laughed softly in her high voice. "Day birds sleep now. All sleep here. Only the owls are awake, watching everything. Watching us. Shh, she's sleeping, but Maude can wake her, if she wants, then you'll see."

Hensley released Maude's hand. "Who's sleeping, Clare? Where?"

"Ancient trees, moonlight and mist, mood all set—perfect." Maude sighed, as a breeze moved wraiths of the thin mist, curling among the huge trees. Then she turned, snapping her fingers. "Wake now, Clare." Maude watched as Clare started and opened her eyes. "Thank you, Clare. Rest now, relax."

Clare stared at the trees, turning around. "Where am I? Maude? Where is this? Hensley, where are we?"

"Uh, where you led us, Clare. You did real good. Spooky. You went to sleep like you do sometimes, while Maude was story-telling, an' we followed you so you wouldn't leave us."

"Oh. Is it all right, Maude?"

"Yes, you did well."

"Spooky?"

"You did very well, Clare." Opening her eyes fully, Maude stepped from the water of the brook onto a faint, overgrown path winding upwards beside the softly chattering brook. The rest followed, murmuring together as they followed the trail though the filtered light of the full moon.

After a few minutes, Maude pushed through a screen of head-high sword fern into a small, grass and flower-carpeted clearing. One immense tree stood alone at one side of the clearing, a little apart from the rest of the grove.

As the troop craned their necks, looking about, Maude took Jeb's hand. "Everyone quiet, join hands and center yourselves. All together, three deep breaths." As they released the last breath with a sigh, Maude began chanting, a series of sounds, words in some nearly forgotten Indian language she had learned. The group joined her chant, beginning softly, slowly building tempo.

The chanting faded into the deep silence of the grove, and the group, again following Maude's example, sat cross-legged on the carpet of fallen needles, grass, and moss. With practiced gestures, they began another type of chant in harmony, eyes open and staring, arms weaving.

In a deep, sing-song, Maude called out above the chant of the others...

Great Mother Earth's tall Sky Pillar
Uplifting the heavens
Open to us, show us your life, your spirit,
    your essence.
Show us your mistress.
Her forest, the great green forest that once was—
It is falling.
Her great trees are dying, the forest is dying.
Call her. Awaken her. Bring her back from her dreams.
Her trees need her. The forest needs her. You need her.
We need her. The world needs her.
Her forest is falling, dying.
Call her. Awaken her. Bring her back.
Bring her back. Bring her back. Bring her back....

That's the way Maude told it to me the next winter, after we got acquainted.

Next morning, sparrows gossiped at each other from a clump of brush near the orange and green painted bus as the sun rose, dimmed by a thin haze. One of the young fellows gave a final blast on a conch shell, its vibration echoing from the hills as a lone buck jumped a pile of slashings and disappeared into the draw below the old logging road. Some of the hippie group stepped down out of the bus and began preparing breakfast on a trestle table set up alongside. Others, including the children, crawled yawning from sleeping bags laid out on the ground or in the vehicles, pulling on clothes in the morning chill. Stretching and talking quietly, some walked toward the brook, others toward the open air latrine. One slender, long-haired man, standing apart on a patch of wild grass near the brook, began playing a wooden flute. The sibilant notes rose above the soft cries of the children. The birds hushed to listen as many of the young people gathered in a circle around the flute player for a morning ritual of stretching and chanting.

Finished, they moved slowly toward the cooking stoves and trestle table, talking softly. Jeb had been watching and now filled a large wooden bowl, holding it out to Maude, but she shook her head and turned, walking up the slope toward the brook and the entrance to the ravine.

Jeb followed her and sat on a rock beside the brook, the bowl of oatmeal in one hand and a paper plate of toast in the other. "Might take awhile for the ritual we did to work, Maude."

"Perhaps, but that ritual and chant were very powerful, the strongest I have ever found in my years of research. Combining material from Native American ritual with that old Greek papyrus scroll, it...oh well, you know that." She sat beside him and took a piece of toast. "That newly discovered scroll, I told you about that, didn't I?" He nodded, chewing.

"So much that was once part of our human heritage has been lost to us. The ancient Greeks especially were so open to all of their experience until the church, and later technology, narrowed their focus. I find it difficult to understand why nothing happened last night."

"Reckon you told me about that other Greek stuff before, too." He turned to look at her, grinning. "Anyway, might take a while, maybe been asleep a real long time. You are some disappointed, Maude?"

"But the planetary patterns are so right. With Pluto in Scorpio, this is a time of great change, a time for uncovering of hidden things. I wish there were more we could do, but we cannot stay longer, we must go south. There is something in today's horoscope I did not understand until a dream last night." She shook her head, braids swinging, then reached for another piece of toast. "I was hoping for at least three days, but the horoscope points south and so did my dream. And I promised the young people they could go to that Rainbow affair next weekend. I thought there would be more time, but it took so long to get the group all together here. They are so disorganized."

"Well, okay. You say it, Maude. South it is."

"Hey, Maude." Hensley joined them. "That was a fine show last night. Big trees hidin' in the mist, an' moonlight, chantin'...great show."

"It was serious, Hensley. And do not speak of those trees anywhere else."

"Sure, Maude, an' without any acid or nothin'. Great! You sure know how to do it, Maude. We gonna do it again tonight?"

"No. We go south this morning. You wanted to go to the gathering."

"Ah, heck, Maude. Let's stay and do some more. Didn't hurt Clare any."

"I promised the others. We will pack up and go south as soon as we can."

When they went back to the asphalt highway late that afternoon, heading south, another man I later met watched them from under the brim of his scuffed leather hat. After they were out of sight, Frank turned away into a clump of old fir trees on the ridge to the east, leaving bare prints with the smooth-soled climber's shoes he always wore.

As the drifting dust settled slowly behind the last of the colorful vehicles, a pair of buzzards settled awkwardly to the ground by the abandoned fire ring, chasing away three crows who flapped off to the west, complaining loudly of life's hassles and injustices, *"Grawk, graw, gaw, gawk, graawk."*

❦

Michael told me some weeks later, at a celebration, how he happened to be in the area the next morning as the sun rose over the coast mountains east of Orick, the southern entrance to Redwood National Park.

A real small place, Orick, with a population of 650. A few gas stations, food stores, lots of souvenir shops. The few houses sit back from the road, and several small herds of cattle graze in fields along the highway and by Redwood Creek that divides the town. Gets pretty fragrant sometimes. Ocean waves, breaking on the headland beside the mouth of the creek can be heard when no cars or trucks are passing, and sometimes a few seagulls cry overhead. Mostly a quiet place.

Michael was driving his fire-engine-red sports car north along the narrow, winding coast highway. He slowed as he rounded the S curve into Orick. As he pulled out of the curve, the motor sputtered, coughed and died, coasting with just enough push to reach the apron of the Exxon gas station on the right.

Michael's a slender fellow, middle height, broad-shouldered, late thirties, brown hair a little thin, clean shaven. Handsome, with dark bedroom eyes, the sort women like. He most always wore new-looking bleached jeans and a denim jacket with the sleeves rolled up. He's usually soft spoken, doesn't swear much, but said he was sure tempted as he levered himself slowly up out of the low car, slammed the door, and stood looking around at the sparse buildings.

"Help you with sumthin', mister? Sumthin' wrong with 'er?" A stooped, gray-haired station attendant walked up, grinning, wiping his hands on a rag.

"Yeah." Michael straightened, drawing a deep breath. "Conked out. Again. Probably the fuel pump. You have a mechanic? Can you fix it?"

"Well...you're right lucky I'm open so early, mister. Don't sleep much anymore. I'm some sort of mechanic. Pretty fancy machine you got here, and if it's the pump, I'll have to send for a replacement most likely. Let's push 'er on into the shop and I'll just check 'er over."

"Well...all right."

The mechanic whistled and after a few minutes, a younger man joined them, helping push the car through the shop door and over the lube lift. The mechanic tossed his rag into a barrel and lifted the hood, whistling softly off key. After looking at the maze of tubes and wires, he pulled a toolkit to the side of the car and took out a wrench. "Try startin' 'er now, mister."

Michael slipped back down into the car and turned the key. The starter whirred. "Yep. Looks like you're right. No gas gettin' in. Try 'er one more time." The starter whirred again. The mechanic straightened, reaching for another rag. "Reckon that's it, mister. Sparks OK, she's not gettin gas. I'll hafta jerk the pump. No small job under all that fancy wiring and all."

Michael climbed out again, slammed the door and stepped to the entrance of the garage, looking at the small town. He turned back again, staring at the mechanic, teeth clenched. "How long?"

"Ah well, kinda hard sayin'. I'll jerk the pump and

check it, an' if that's the trouble, I'll need send to the city for another." The station attendant scratched his grease-streaked neck, looking at the ceiling with a solemn expression. "Might have it done in four days, if they send the rebuilt pump on the Greyhound bus right away. An' if they got one in stock, which they may. May have to send to the factory though. Yeah, four days, all goes well."

Michael continued staring at the mechanic, then turned again, looking at the small town. "Just fix it. Okay?" Stepping to the back of the car, he unlocked the trunk and tugged a large royal-blue pack loose from the narrow space. Pulling it out he set it against the bumper. "Was going hiking, inland in the Marbles, guess I'll hike here instead. Take a week if you need it."

He finished packing some things from the car, jammed a straw hat on his head and without looking back, shouldered the pack and started toward the road.

"Mister! I'll need you sign the work order 'fore you leave."

Michael stopped, took another deep breath, and followed the mechanic back into the station. Five minutes later, he headed north through the sleepy town, a red sleeping pad bouncing against the royal-blue pack.

"Thank you, mister Michael Duggan. I'll have 'er fixed within the week."

In winter the ancient redwood forest of the park is mysterious with rain, drifting fog, and the fragrances of wet plants, but summer days, while often overcast, are mostly dry and dusty. This day, the highway through the park was cool, with green shade gently pierced by slanting shafts of bright light. Michael told me later how he noticed the sunlight creating ghostly mosaics on the smooth black asphalt as he walked north along the highway.

By mid-afternoon, tiring, he stopped by the same dirt

logging road that led to Maude's campsite and shrugged out of his big pack, laying it against a tree bole rising from a bed of fern beside the highway. Holding his straw hat in one hand while wiping his forehead and thinning hair with a hanky, he watched the ungainly motor homes cruise past. Driving along the highway, I've often seen them. Always seemed strange to me, having small houses rolling around on wheels. They ought to stay put.

Shrugging into the pack again with a groan, Michael looked back at the westering sun, shook his head, and headed east up the side of the road, stepping between the puddles and ribbons of dust.

Later, I came along with Buck in the company's big green dump truck, towing a low-boy trailer loaded with a big yellow Caterpillar tractor. It's a heavy load to be dragging behind and I slowed to a crawl before turning off the pavement onto that same dirt road. Shifting up again, gaining speed, I saw a flash of color ahead on the narrow road and hit the brakes. The trailer wheels locked, skidding and bouncing as we stopped. A rising cloud of dust swirled past the cab, glowing in a shaft of sunlight as a pair of buzzards flapped heavily into the air from beside the road. Guess they were feeding on roadkill. Happens a lot around here. Animals never seem to learn.

As I waited, the colorful vehicles I had glimpsed a ways ahead came around the curve. Guess Buck wasn't feeling too good that day, hadn't been saying much, but now he straightened and tipped his yellow hardhat back, rubbing his forehead. "Goddamned hippies, what in hell, Joe." Buck is a catskinner I worked with a lot of the time, early forties, blonde, a little shorter than I am, but square built. He most times likes to talk as I drive him to work and back to the shop.

"Shouldn't of drank that last pitcher of Coors last night, ya know? Hell! Run over 'em, Joe."

I was sitting back, one foot on the power brake, watching the oncoming vehicles. "Likely the group that big deputy warned us about. Yeah, there comes that odd bus. Guess I better pull us over to the side a bit more, they might not be too sober either." Black exhaust rolled from the twin stacks, mixing with the brown dust as we rolled slowly forward, crawling along the edge of the dirt road, stopping again.

"First it's the damn, dirty, leg-spreading hippies like this bunch, then them snobbish college-skewed mother-loving environmentalists. Now Earth First crazies. Probably some in this group. Where in hell'll it end, Joe?"

"Well this bunch is leaving. Likely just hippies, no spikers or tree sitters. Wonder what they've been doing back in there?"

"Hell, you know as well as I do. Fornicating, smoking pot, chanting, meditating, singing, all that crazy stuff they like. Parasites think this is a Garden of Eden or something. Sing and play all day and somebody else can pay the bills. Ought to run 'em all off."

The curiously painted vehicles stopped alongside, waiting on the lead van's turn onto the highway, and I started slowly forward, the motor bellowing as I worked the gears. "How come you know so much about them, Buck?"

"All right, wise guy, so I read a book 'bout 'em. I may be a hardhat, redneck, dozer jockey, but I can read. Just curious, you know? Like to know what's going on. Saw something 'bout them on TV, too. Okay?" He pushed his hardhat back again, rubbing his forehead and scowling.

"Sure, Buck."

"Yeah. Well, somebody's got to do something before those hotshots make the whole area a National Park or Wilderness or something else crazy. Those mother's snobs been slapping appeals on everything we try to do. Then those damned saboteurs come along spiking trees and trashing the equipment. Damn Congress ought to do something, 'fore we all lose our jobs. Hell, my cousin down in the mill's getting real worried, another baby coming and all. He's real worried. Hospital bills going up, everything going to hell. Working man's getting shafted every which way. No end to it, Joe. You and me'll be okay for a while, working for the company. They'll still need roads built, but what are the loggers and mill fellas gonna do when the logs are all gone or tied up in parks and wilderness and such? Ain't fair, ya know?"

"The government and mill owners and all will work out something. All we have to worry about right now is getting your tractor in to the next job."

Buck stretched, turning to a new position in the cab of the dumptruck as he unscrewed the cup of his big Thermos. "Boss tell you why we're going out here? Something for Barron? No redwoods left to cut out this way. Took them all years ago. About the time I came west."

"Wants a new road run on to the east. Doug fir on the ridge. Mr. Barron's in a hurry to get that last stand logged out."

"Hell. I've put roads all over this area and that's bad. East of here's all up and down like everything got set on edge, then melted a little. Rough country. Cost a bundle, putting a road in there. Dumb bet."

We rolled past a hiker half-hidden behind a big royal-blue pack, walking along the edge of the road. I watched in the rearview as he turned away until the worst of the roiling cloud of dust had passed, then wearily lifted one fist toward us, middle finger extended. Looked like he wasn't much used to hiking back roads. Used to get that a lot in the late summer with hikers wandering all over. "Don't know the answers, Buck. Redwood, fir, not many big trees left around here where anybody can get to them. Like you say, rough country. Makes the trees more valuable. Let's just deliver your Cat."

The rooster-tail of dust caught up with us as I shifted into the truck's lowest gear and slowed as the road turned up a steep, eroded gully. We topped out below the logged-over slope at the end of the road and parked. Buck put down his Thermos and climbed out on his side as I shut off the motor, set the brake, and got out.

I spread two maps on the low trailer. "Found this old map shows a small canyon over there in that hillside. Guess this one's not accurate. Sure don't see any canyon. Shows a homestead right here too, somebody name of McEvoy. Whole 160 acres. Anyway, we go by the new map." I pointed to the other. "Boss said to grade out a new road that way, to the fir on the ridge. Like you say, going to be an expensive bit of road, but that's what the boss said. Better hustle and get your tractor off, if we want to be back by quitting time so you can join the fellows at the beer hall."

Buck settled his hardhat and picked up a bar to release the tiedowns. "Yeah, ol' Barron Mills, Inc. The BM hisself, he's a tough bird. If he wants those trees, he'll get them. Ever meet him, Joe?"

"Was in his office once. Reminded me of that TV show, Star Trek. All chrome and plastic furniture, computers, and blinking lights. I'll give you a hand off-loading your tractor and you can fix this first bit of road. I'll move the trailer up when you're finished, and meantime, I'll walk up and check on the old survey stakes. Surveyor should be here any time to lay out the rest of it, but don't need to wait on him."

"Righto, Joe-boy. Good thing one of us is thinking clear today. Get my big lady off her tow-trailer, then watch our dust. DC umteen Caterpillar tractor, I love you. Yore my faithful baby!"

"Anybody would think this bulldozer was your true love for sure."

"Power, man, don't you know. When I get my Adrian

going, nothing stops us. Some mountains might slow us a while, but nothing stops us. Same when I get rich. Real power. Just push everything out of my way. That's living. Like ol' Barron hisself."

I shook my head, picked up another bar and started loosening the tie-downs on my side. "I'll admit you handle a dozer better than anyone I've seen. A for-sure catskinner. Maybe it is true love." I had to laugh. "There. Your big yellow lover-baby's loose."

"Righto, Joe-boy, love it is. We'll be up that ridge in no time. No time at all." The diesel coughed and roared to life, clanking down the ramped trailer. Turning toward the eroded roadway, Buck waved as the machine moved ponderously forward and, half laughing, he began singing at the top of his voice, "What ever Barron wants, Barron gets, BM will never be denied...".

❦

INTERLUDE: While Joe knows all the rest of the story, one part he never heard was what happened in Mr. Barron's high-tech office on the second floor of a wood-sided, A-frame building on a low rise above the sprawling lumber mill.

A picture window fills most of one wall and looks down on the mill and the small town across the four-lane highway. Steam and smoke rise from the mill's forest of chimneys in tall, swirling columns, flattening and spreading to the south above the encircling hills.

Alone in his wood-paneled office, Barron sits at his broad steel desk dialing the phone. As he waits, he leans back in his padded swivel chair, jacket off, necktie loose, one arm over his balding head.

"Jane, how is life treating you? How is everything down at the California Department of Forestry? I heard that you folks had quite a blowout at your picnic last week. You have a good time?...

"Yes, you are right. I am really sorry I missed it. Too busy, you know how it is. Next time I'll be there for sure....

"Right!" He laughs without change of expression. "Yes please, I would like to talk with Forester Smith, if he's not too busy....

"John, Bart Barron here. You have a minute?...

"Right. I'm sorry I missed your party, heard it was a real good one....

"Right. Wanted to tell you I've got the boys working on extending that logging road into the stand of fir east of the park over in section fifty-one. Logging crew will go in and cut them next week. No problems, and I want you to know that I surely do appreciate your support for getting those trees, and for getting the Harvest Timber Plan through so quickly....

"That's right. And I wanted to ask if you'd heard anything more about that redwood grove over in forty-nine?...

"Gone? Somebody bought the grove to preserve it? I was afraid that might happen. Seems like that happens a lot more these days....

"No, no. I know you did all you could to hold it out for us....

"We're getting desperate over here. If we can't find more big trees soon, we'll have to start laying off men. Can't be helped. You know we're set up for big logs only. No big logs, no work. Tough on the workers and their families. I sure hate to see them get into hard times when most the rest of the country's doing so well....

"I know they sometimes overrule you in Sacramento, but we have to get them to understand our situation up here. We've got a lot of families and the whole local economy depending on the mill continuing at full capacity....

"You understand. You've always been very helpful, John, and we need your help to get the message through to your superiors. And to the legislature. They've got to understand our situation also....

"I know you're doing all you can and believe me I really appreciate your efforts. I sure won't forget....

"Right. Well, we'll just have to keep trying for those trees over in section fifty-one, and we'll keep our eyes open for any more that might become available anywhere in the area....

"Really do appreciate your understanding, John. Really do. Keep in touch, okay? Bye."

Leaning forward, frowning, Barron hangs up the phone, then straightens and swings about to the amber computer monitor at his side. Punching keys, he calls up another list and more figures as the phone rings and his secretary enters with a sheaf of papers.

❦

2

THE AWAKENING

...Everything that happened last fall was hushed, so you likely never heard of Weitchie, but you do know about the coast Redwood groves; everybody has seen them, or pictures of them. That's what this story is really about, the great trees, Sequoia Sempervirens, *Maude called them. For me that's become a special name.*

But it's hard telling about things that most people wouldn't believe, even if they saw for themselves, and most of what happened was like that, real different. And Weitchie herself, so full of life, Maude called her a Nature Spirit. How do I tell you about that, the very heart of the forest? What words can I use? Guess it's better just getting on with the story.

Michael was making hard going of it with that big pack when he gave us the finger as we passed him on the dusty old logging road. He and I didn't get on very good at first, but like I said, people tell me things and Michael told me later how he met Weitchie in her grove while he was bathing in a pool. Washing the dust off. Guess he was em-bare-assed. Weitchie was naked too, seems she never was much for wearing clothes...

It was dusky-rose twilight as Michael limped past the big tractor and its trailer that Buck and I had left parked at the end of the road. Breathing hard and looking around, he stopped to scoop a drink from the brook. Then he walked along it, stumbling through the grass and brush until he saw the blackened firepit beside the rotting stump. Taking off his shoes, he began limping about, pulling gear out of his pack and laying it out for the night on a grassy flat spot: brown plastic ground cloth, red pad and sleeping bag, food bag, inflatable pillow. Michael's kind of a fussy sort, but I guess he was too tired to put up his little yellow tent. When he had it all arranged, he started up his tiny, howling backpacking stove on a flat rock beside the firepit, and scooping water from the brook in a small billy, prepared supper while a gentle breeze fluffed his hair.

As the moon rose over the treetops on the ridge to the east several hours after sunset, Michael slipped out of his sleeping bag, still sound asleep, and walked a weaving path toward the moon and the brush-screened ravine between the two rock outcrops. Slipping to his hands and knees in the cold water of the brook, he woke with a cry, jumped out of the water onto the dusty wild grass and stood for a long moment, rubbing his eyes, looking quickly about in the silent, moonlit night, shaking his head. He said there was a big horned owl in a stunted, half-dead sapling on the slope that must have been watching him. As he started back toward the campsite, an animal went crashing through the brush down the draw.

Walking slowly to a bush, he started to relieve himself but jumped as the owl called his 'whooo, whooo,' floating by overhead. As he was walking back toward his tumbled sleeping bag, careful of his bare, blistered feet, Michael heard a scratching sound and a low growl. He stopped, staring, as two raccoons scurried away from his food sack. Putting the torn sack under his head, he lay down facing away from the moonlight, and, pulling the bag over his head, fell asleep again.

When Michael told me about all of this, he said that before he stumbled and woke up in the cold water of the brook, he had been having a dream of flowers, animals, tall trees, and a naked young woman. Said the dream was like his old favorite movie, *Fantasia*, but more erotic. Guess he didn't pay much attention to his dream, right away.

Next morning soon after dawn, two jays woke Michael as they raucously scolded each other from a sapling pine growing on the hillside. Buck and I were just starting work about then, and that tractor's noisy. For a while, Michael just sat on his bag, staring at the two rock outcrops and the clump of salal. Then he pulled on clothes and started up his roaring little stove.

I didn't see him there at first, behind that stump, and I guess he didn't like all the noise we made, because first I did see of him, he had packed up his gear and was trudging off toward the near ridge to the east. I could have told him it was real rough country that way if he had stopped to talk. Anyway, I was working so I didn't think much about it.

Michael returned, limping, as Buck and I stopped for lunch the next day. After he put down his pack, we saw him wandering about, picking up and dropping pieces of wood and small stones, then stopping and watching as we started back to work on the new section of road. He finally shook his head, dropped the weathered stick in his hands, and walked rapidly to the top of the shallow slope, to the clump of brush growing there over the brook. I couldn't see him after that, but he told me later he hung his shoes over one shoulder, stepped into the water, and pushed through the clump of salal, taller than a man, filling the narrow space between the two crumbling rock outcrops.

Coming out the other side, he continued up the tumbling, rocky brook until he rounded a corner in the narrow ravine. He stopped, staring at the mist shrouded trees and flowering bushes filling the canyon before him. He told me the air was full of birdsong, fragrance of flowers, and sounds of scurrying small animals. There was so much life and color there in the rays of sunlight slanting through the trees that he just stood and stared for a while. I did the same when I first saw that narrow canyon and the grove of ancient redwoods. It would stop anybody.

Coming back to himself, Michael stepped onto the moss-carpeted bank of the brook, and putting his shoes back on, followed the dim trail winding between the bushes, clumps of fern, and boles of the great trees. As he pushed through the screen of fern into the tree-circled clearing, he stopped to watch two does grazing six yards away on the other side. They lifted their heads, looked at him indifferently, then returned to feeding.

Michael walked on into the clearing as an iridescent, blue-green hummingbird hovered before his eyes for a moment, explored his red-checked shirt, then darted away as another looked him over, then another. A black-stippled orange butterfly landed on his arm, then fluttered away in pursuit of another, smaller one. Standing well back from beneath the biggest tree, he ran his eyes up its trunk from shoulder-high buttress roots to the top, rising green into the cobalt-blue sky. Looking down again, a thick burl forming a half-umbrella between two of the buttress roots caught his eye. The burl shielded a deep, shadowed opening in the side of the huge trunk. Shaking his head Michael turned back to retrieve his pack and set up his yellow tent among the flowers and clumps of grass in the clearing.

Later, squatting on a flat rock ankle deep in a small pool of the brook, splashing the cold water on himself for a bath, he noticed the horned owl watching him. As he looked back, he heard a woman's soft laugh close by like a chime tinkling.

"Who's there? Hey, who laughed? C'mon, not fair sneaking up while a fellow's taking a bath. Where are you?" Again the tinkling laugh. Turning slowly to his left, Michael noticed an iridescent blue lizard doing pushups in a shaft of sunlight on a rock. "It wasn't you, fella. Who's here?"

A slight noise behind him and as he turned, he slipped, falling into the small pool. Sputtering and thrashing back to his feet, he wiped his eyes, staring at a naked young woman with shoulder length red hair standing between two bushes growing out of the half-rotten tree trunk that dammed the pool. She was bent over, laughing silently.

"Hey, that's not fair. That's not...my God, BB! Where did you come from? But you can't be. Who are you?"

Stilling her laughter, she sat on the soft bark of the downed tree, dangling tiny feet over the pool, looking at him mischievously.

"To my home welcome be, handsome man. And to the water of my bathing pool, though too cold for you it may be." She laughed again, then sobered. "Welcome, yes. My place this. Weitchie I am. You are who?"

"I don't believe any of this. You're too beautiful, and out here in the woods...it can't be." He shook his head. "I'm Michael, from the Bay Area. Where did you come from, Weechee?"

"Ah, Mik-ail, for my ears a nice sound. Come from other place I do not. Only from my mother tree waken, finding a strange man in my pool with his hands splashing himself." She grinned again. "The water, so terribly cold is? The water you all red-skinned make?"

"Yes it is, pretty cold. I, well, if it's okay, I'd like to come out. Before I freeze my...I'm really cold!"

"'Ok-ay,' what is? 'Bay Area,' what is?"

"Please. It really is cold. Do you mind?"

"Come out, if so cold you are. Not cold here." She patted the soft, deeply furrowed bark of the downed tree beside herself. "Something in cold water hold you? A 'BB,' what is?"

Slipping on the mossy rock of the pool bottom, Michael pulled himself out onto the log. "I really don't believe any of this. My God, ears like a miniature Spock! For all the wild places they got to, the Enterprise was sure never like this. And eyes like soft, shiny red carnelian. Where did you ever get contact lenses like that?" He hurriedly wiped water from his hair, arms and legs, half turning away from her. "You must be from Hollywood, no one could really look like that." He laughed, half nervously. "C'mon. Who put you up to this. How'd anybody know I was here? I didn't know I was coming here myself, just wandered in a couple of hours ago. Didn't see anyone out on the road. No cars. How'd you get here?"

She stiffened, turning away, smile fading. "I not so good understand you. The manner of speaking of your kind while I sleep so much changed has." She looked away, eyes unfocused for a long minute, then looked at him again. "I too long sleep. So much changed!" She turned, facing Michael, face serious. "As my mother, so I also am looking. My eyes and ears you so much trouble?" She raised one hand to an ear, brushing the red hair back. "Other man like me."

"I'm sorry. I really didn't mean to be rude, you're very beautiful. Exotic. But you know that, hell's bells, a backpacker's dearest fantasy come alive. How could I ask for more? And please understand, I'm not ungrateful, it's just that some of my friends and family have a wicked and sometimes perverted sense of humor. You really must admit this is a little bit on the heavy side. C'mon, who are you really? You're very beautiful and I would like to get to know you, but who put you up to this? Meeting me here, well, naked and everything, here in this hidden grove. Please tell me."

"You humans with own eyes not believe what you see." She shook her head, tossing her mane of red hair back and accompanying her words with gestures and movement. "Always suspicious. No joy with such, not have good, full life so. Who I am, I am. Here I live. Always, since my mother, after my birthing, leave me so. A 'Hollywood,' is what? And a 'BB'? Of these things tell me so I may learn the way in this time of your speaking. Long time I sleep. Tell me."

"So, okay. Whatever the movie is, I'll go along, you're much too lovely to resist. But don't you, uh, have any clothes?" Weitchie laughed again. "Well maybe you don't need them, but I do. I'm not used to...well I always had a weakness for red hair. Especially...does something to me that's embarrassing with a stranger. Uh, let me get my clothes, and I have a spare clean shirt. Nice flannel. I was just going to put it on myself." Michael stood and easing over a low azalea shrub, reached to a nearby salmonberry bush and picked up a purple plaid shirt, tossing it to her. Still half laughing at him, she put it on as he, still damp, slipped into his dusty shirt and jeans.

"That's better...or maybe not. Would you mind buttoning it up all of the way, please. Thank you." Michael found a dry spot and reseated himself.

"You want me to talk awhile? Then you'll tell me what this is all about and who you are and where you come from?"

Weitchie nodded, serious again. "Yes, your talk I must hear. I learn quickly the words to rightly use. For my kind our way is."

"Well okay. For starters, you reminded me of BB. That's Brigitte Bardot. We—you know how it is—young men, when they first become sexually mature, they fantasize a lot. At least I did. Bardot was a French movie star, very sexy. I used to daydream about her a lot."

"Blushing you are, Mik-ail. Beautiful she must be. Like her much you do?"

"Well, used to be very sexy at least. I actually dreamed about her in my night dreams for several years. When I first saw you, it was like those dreams again. Even standing in that cold water, I couldn't help reacting like I was a teenager again. The shape of your face, your lips, your body, that red hair— kind of embarrassing, cold water or not. Now I see you better you are really much more beautiful. She was just a fantasy."

She smiled. "Thank you Mik-ail. 'Okay,' what is?"

"Okay is like all right, everything fine. I'll bet your eyes are really a light blue. That red hair surely can't be faked, not all over, even your arms and legs...so your eyes have to be blue. Or maybe green? Nobody has eyes like red carnelian marbles, though it is a great idea. Really goes with your hair, your coloring. You have to be from Hollywood. Right?"

"What is 'Hollywood,' Mik-ail?"

"Okay. Hollywood is a place south of here where they make up fantasy stories to entertain people. Some who live there can't tell the difference—not sure I can right now. Anyway, it's a place where a lot of people live who do things like that."

"They stories for telling make?"

"Yeah, and pictures and music to go with the stories. Can't we talk about you? I would really like to know you."

Weitchie sighed. "Very much changed has. Please tell me why they all my trees take." She gestured with one arm. "But these few, all other trees gone are. With joy for my great forest I wake and I call of love send, but my forest answers not. From my forest all life is gone. Why it is so?" Her eyes glistened. "I know as you come here you must see. Trees are gone. Much of death I feel. Why is it so? What you humans do?"

Michael frowned and turned away looking around for a moment, then back. "You, somehow, sort of own the forest here? All of it?"

A tear streaked one cheek, trembling on her narrow chin. "Yes. By even human-made law, this my place. All, as far as a high-flying feathered cousin can see, all me, mine. Mik-ail, you saw, my trees gone are. Some earth turnings before now, when I look trees well are. Now I wake and trees gone are. So fast gone. Other waking, from high seeing place of winged cousin, all land with trees covered. South, same my sisters. North, same for other sisters. East, different sisters, not what you call redwood, but all places low and high with trees covered. Now only few by great water still. And few to sun rising. Others all gone. Why? What you human people do?"

"Well I guess they needed the lumber. For fences, picnic tables, I don't know really what they make out of redwood lumber. Decks, I guess."

"I not know these things, 'fence,' 'deck,' what is?"

Michael took a deep breath. "Well, a fence is to divide property so...keep in dogs and kids and such like. A deck is like on the back of a house, so people can sit in the sun, barbecue, cook outdoors."

"They use my trees for food heat?"

"Uh, not exactly. How long have you been gone, Weechee?"

"Your kind count turnings of earth, that I remember. We do not. How many turnings I know not. I think many, very many." Michael looked at her for a long moment then sighed. "You say you live here and own these trees, but you have been gone a long time?"

"Yes, in Dream Time. With my people, I sleep. In these times, such our way. Sometime sleep long, very long as human count."

"Like Rip Van Winkle maybe? You've been sleeping for decades? Or are you telling me you are not even human? Oh c'mon, you're much too beautiful to be an ET or a fairy or whatever. Got to have a better story than that." He chuckled. "And I would really like to know you. Can't we..."

Weitchie stood, wiping her eyes and looking down at him for a long moment. "When I in Earth Time before am, when I waken, human believe me. Now...so much changed." She shivered.

"What was it like, what was happening when you were last in 'Earth Time'? Last here in your grove?"

"I with human man speak last when many men through forest come, along ways where waters flow." She gestured all about, turning. "Round pan have. Swish about for what you call gold. Hard men. They come, they look everywhere, they most leave. One man, name McEvoy, stay. Good man, he say he make all good so other man not trouble here, my forest. He stay til life leave him. He teach me your tongue speak so. My grove here safe still, but must make all of forest again new. Not good, all gone. Too much of death."

"These men, they all came on foot. No cars?"

"What is 'cars'?"

"You're saying they were prospectors, Forty-Niners?. That was a long time ago, more than a hundred years. You've been sleeping since the prospectors were searching for gold all over California?"

"No. Some times wake, love my trees. Maybe so many turnings pass as fingers and toes. Not say words with human man since McEvoy. It is so."

"Oh, come on. I really would rather get to know you. Please?"

"My friend McEvoy, a word for me said. Dryad. He called me so. Dryad of redwood forest. He say old Greek word for my kind."

"Ooh...that's it! A dryad! Great!" Michael could hardly talk for laughing. He said he almost fell off the log. "You really are an actress, and a very good one. All the way back to the ancient Greeks yet. Great idea. It would have taken me hours to figure that out. Who would think of the Greeks in a scene like the redwoods. Truly some of my friends, and my family, have strange imaginations. A dryad! Where are the cameras? Where..."

Half sobering, Michael looked up, wiping his eyes. Weitchie was gone. The large horned owl glided silently over the pool and a moment later sounded a 'who-oo, who-oo,' from the forest. "Weechee, wait, please. Weechee. Where are you? Please Weechee..."

Michael was really shook, finding her gone, so sudden like that.

❦

It seems like Maude and Jeb had a hard time getting anything done or going anywhere with that bunch of young hippies. Every one of them had different ideas about most everything, but Maude and Jeb got them a ways south by Thursday evening, and they spent the night at a campground in young redwoods down in Marin county. Maude told me later she felt uneasy and had tried a trance ceremony with Clare that evening, but Clare only mumbled about tall trees, a short dark man with long arms, and another man who was sleeping, though awake and walking about. She said Clare cried a lot and was badly disturbed in trance, so Maude didn't want to push her. None of that made any sense to me, and I guess it didn't Maude either because she said she hadn't slept real well that night and had some strange dreams.

The next morning was cool and overcast there in the

middle of Marin and while the others fixed breakfast, Maude got out her Astrology stuff and studied for a while, then sat back in the van and stared at the trees.

"Breakfast, Maude." Jeb held the wooden bowl out to her.

She looked up at him, eyes slowly focusing, then took the bowl. "We must go back, Jeb. Something is not as it should be."

"Back?"

"Yes. To that camping site off Highway 101. Back to the hidden redwood grove where we did the ceremony Sunday."

Jeb raised his eyebrows. "Young folk counting on the gathering."

"I know. I will talk with them." Setting the bowl down, Maude rose and walked to the circle of young people and children eating their breakfast, standing quietly watching them until she had their attention.

"We must return to the redwoods where we did the ceremony. I feel that something is happening there, something I must learn about." A chorus of protests arose from the troop. "I know, I promised you could attend the Rainbow gathering, but something has changed."

Hensley stood up, mouth half full. "Ah, come on Maude, we got to go. If we don't, they'll never meet us." Some laughed while others agreed with Hensley.

"I am sorry, but I must return to the redwoods immediately."

"I'll come with you, Maude." Clare's soft voice filled a momentary silence. The rest immediately raised more objections, all talking at once. Maude held up one hand, smiling at them and waiting until they quieted.

"I may have tried to do too much, too many things at once. Or perhaps we were meant to leave for a time, but I feel we must return to that hidden grove, and quickly. The ceremony we performed there is somehow not complete, something more needs to be done. Those who must go on, who have promised to be at the gathering, may do so and we can come together again another day. You all have my mailing address and answering service number. I will leave a message there for you."

"I want to stay with you, Maude."

"Ah Clare, let's go on to the gatherin'. You promised."

"Didn't, Hensley. I didn't promise. Always said I would stay with Maude."

"Oh, all right. Guess I'll stay with Maude and Jeb too, otherwise you won't be with me."

With just four of them, it didn't take long to pack up and head back north.

❦

Michael told me later how shook up he was as he searched the small grove through the rest of that day and the next morning. He found no one. Small animals of all sorts, birds, butterflies, but no person. Said he looked all through the narrow canyon, at first hardly noticing the bright sunshine, flowers and birds, just wandering around the grove for hours. Guess he is sort of a dreamer anyway, a romantic, and meeting Weitchie like that...tough for a city fellow. I can believe he was upset, fell for her real hard. I'll sure never forget the first time I met her, and she had clothes on then. Maybe an Indian might have been able to believe her, somebody like that, seems like they're more open to that sort of thing than we are.

He finally walked out the next morning, just before noon, and watched Buck and me for a while until we stopped for lunch. I was going to speak with him then, but he was gone. The company liked us to be polite to hikers and tourists, help them if they need anything. But he was gone so Buck and I just ate, then went back to work.

He told me after we met how he went back into the canyon and sat on a half-rotten log beside the waterfall watching tiny rainbows flash as drops of spray caught the sun. After a while he lay back and fell asleep.

"Mik-ail. Talk with me more."

He slowly sat up, looking at her standing beside a salmonberry bush. Remembering, she buttoned the shirt. "Weechee! I'm sorry if I said something wrong. Thank you for coming back, but where did you go? I'm sorry I laughed, but it seemed so funny, so clever, just the sort of thing my brother and cousins would think of. Honest, I didn't mean to offend you. I very much want to know you. Tell me what I did wrong."

"Is okay, Mik-ail. Sad for my trees I am. Maybe patience is not long with me now for always trees they are here, my great trees, now are gone. And my sisters, I cannot hear. Cannot reach to them, cannot leave this small place. Understand I do not. My trees, they so long live, could not all die so soon."

"I'm sorry, Weechee. I don't know anything about logging or timber or forests, I just come out to hike when the city gets to me. You know how it is, a person has to get out of the city once in a while. But I don't understand very well about your living here and these being your trees and all. Perhaps I could help somehow, if you would tell me all about yourself. I don't like seeing you sad. Please tell me."

"You will not believe." Weitchie shook her head with a toss, throwing the fine strands of red hair away from her face as she sat beside him.

'Honest, I'll try. Whatever you want to tell me. I know I was wrong yesterday. There's no one else been here, so it's not a movie at least. I thought maybe cameras were..." He shrugged his shoulders and grinned at her. "No cameras." At her expression, he sobered again. "I'm sorry, honest. Please tell me all about yourself. Tell me how you come to be here, and everything."

Holding her feet out in the spray of the waterfall, she looked at him for a long moment, then turned, picking up a rabbit that nuzzled her thigh, stroking his soft back and sides. "I try turn words same like you human in this time. You are not first human coming here in this time, some other were here only two turnings before you. You of them know? Strong woman with others?" He shook his head. "For me made strong call, woke me from Dream Time where I go with my kind for many turnings. I wake, send out joy to my forest and all life here, but death answer. Beyond this small place of mother tree only death answer. I must forest new make. Forest life my life is. Must new make." She put the rabbit down, looking at him intensely.

"Sure, Weechee. I understand. It is sad that so many trees have been cut. Tragic, really. It bothered me when I walked in past all the stumps, but that's the way the world is now. We try to save some, but..."

"For making new beginning, I am called Weitchie."

"Okay. Witchee, better, Sorta like witchy?"

"More near. Wee-et-chia."

"Wee-et-chia, okay? That is a beautiful name. Just right for you."

"Yes. In my realness, everything right is. And, I am dryad. As my mother before me. From the beginning of all that is on great mother earth have been trees. My kind when we first awaken in Earth Reality, we make one with trees."

"Okay, Weitchie. Will you tell me about being a dryad?" Michael turned, shifting closer.

"I am life and what you call reality of forest. Such words my friend, you call prospector, McEvoy, gave me when I wake in his time. I think he very wise, also what you call poet." She shrugged, tossing her red hair back off her shoulders. "For me, I am. Not more, not less. I am.

And I am my trees, my forest, all life in forest is me. That is more how you would say?"

"Yes, that's the way some talk nowadays. Or close enough. I also like the way you were talking. Everything about you is wonderful. You have lived here, among these trees, all your life then?"

She looked at him for a long moment, then stood from the moss-spangled log, taking his hand. "Come. I show more."

Michael followed her between the pink flowering rhododendron, berry-laden bushes and ferns, back to the largest tree, towering over the clearing.

She led him to the opening beneath the overhanging burl. "Here my home place, here in mother tree. She keep me while I live in Dream Time. She close opening and feed me, give me all. You see?"

"You sleep in this opening in the tree? And the tree feeds you?"

"Yes. You will see, I not need eat like you. Tree feed while I sleep. Each day so. I am made so. How you say, my reality is so. Opening in tree is only enough for small one like me, but you see."

"Does your family live near here, your mother, does she..."

Stepping away from the tree and looking unfocused into the distance, Weitchie frowned, anger in her eyes for a moment. Then, with a wordless cry she dropped to her knees, collapsing to the flower-strewn grass, crying.

"Weitchie, please. What did I say? I'm sorry. Don't go away again, please." Michael knelt beside the trembling figure, then lay beside her, taking her in his arms. She turned, burying her head in his shoulder, sobbing.

He stroked her hair and back until she slowly quieted. "I'm sorry, Weitchie. I don't understand, but I want to. Honest, I really do want to know you. I want to understand. Please be patient with me."

She pushed back a little, looking into his eyes, then snuggled up again, pressing against him, rubbing her damp face against his flannel shirt.

"Ummm."

"Uh, isn't the ground a little hard?" She shook her head, hair tickling his chin. "You're so beautiful. I'm not very comfortable lying together like this. That shirt, and I..."

"Is okay, Mik-ail. Is good you like me and your hard male place press against me so strong. Is very good." She wriggled lower along his body, then rolled back, undoing her shirt buttons and reaching for his.

Naturally Michael didn't give me a lot of detail about the two of them when he told me all of this; he wouldn't; he was too much of a gentleman, but I was married once for awhile, so I guess I can fill in how it was. All he said was they fell in love real quick. Said she was an armful. If she was as lively making love as she was just talking, I can sure believe it. Always moving and using her body to express herself. Guess that's what they mean by body language. After the two of them were finished, they talked again.

"I'm sorry I made you sad again, Weitchie, honest, I'll try to understand. When I get back to the city I'll look up dryads and find out all I can. I'll— God!—I don't want to wake up from this and go back to the city! Not now."

Weitchie sat up in the flannel shirt, running fingers through her hair. "Awake you are, Mik-ail. I am real. You see, no?" She poked him in the ribs.

"Ouch! I know I'm awake, only...sort of not awake. This is too good, can't be really real."

"I want very much you not go away to city place. Much need I have for you, Mik-ail. I need friend help me understand how so much has changed. So much changed." For a moment her face clouded, then touching his hair, she smiled again. "You like me, Mik-ail, you like lie with me?" She ran the fingers of one hand through her hair, then held out a finger for a hummingbird. The tiny iridescent red bird hovered for a moment, then landed, wings stilled and she stroked its back with one finger. "The little ones like my red color. They think they maybe find sweet nectar from me."

"Oh lady, you can't know how much I like you. I've never met anyone even the least like you, not near so beautiful and warm. Sweet? Oh, Weitchie."

"You like me more than your BB?"

He snorted, pulling her down beside him again as the tiny bird darted away. "She was only a dream. You...I still don't understand what you are, but I know I don't want to leave you. Not now."

"Is good, for I am dryad and female. Such a female a strong male need. All dryad are female, all female need male, no? Same all life."

"Yes. All of life, male and female. Never appreciated it so much before." He slid one hand under the plaid shirt, stroking her back. "And I need you."

Later, they stood on rocks in the small pool, splashing each other as birds, butterflies, lizards, and a pair of squirrels joined in their play. Weitchie pushed Michael into the deeper water, but as he fell, he caught one arm and pulled her in with him. He quickly stood, wiping the water from his hair. "God, this water is cold. How do you stand it?"

"Is very nice water. Human man soft now. Not so man of past."

"You're right about that. They were supposed to be a real tough bunch. I want to warm up." He climbed out of the pool, finding a smooth rock in sunlight beside the mossy log. She came out too, laying back on the moss and warm bark beside him, plucking a toadstool and munching on it.

He sighed, then chuckled. "You know, when my car broke down, in that other world, I left it not caring if I ever went back. Or lived another week. I just wanted to get lost in the forest and never find my way back. Kinda scares me now, when I think of it."

"Life not good for you Mik-ail? Not have joy in city place life? Is special place here. Make all good for you. Let all sorrow and anger and dark feeling go into rock beneath you. Let all go."

"Yes. Umm. I think you're right. Everything's very different here. You even smell different."

"You mean different from many human woman you know."

"I haven't known so many."

"Is okay, all different now. I know from my friend before, McEvoy, you and your kind have not place, no root set deep in earth. You drift like seed of bright yellow dandelion. Fly before winds, this way, that way. Not so for me. For my kind is different, I am place and place is me. I have not life apart from place, only Dream Time. Trees, birds, animals and all here this place, all me. Your kind sometime like tiny mayfly, here, there, gone. Not good, live so fast, Better for all you be calm, quiet, have place, live much more long time."

"Yes, it might be you're right. Can I stay with you? Here?"

"Oh yes, I want it so. But you need understand me. I need man help make my forest new." She sat up, turning to lean over him. "I need have strong mate, have male seed in me, all forest make new so."

"Tell me more."

"We, my kind, made for us different reality from human kind. We live in bodies when we wish, leave them sleeping in trees or other safe place when we dream. But now want, must, make forest all new again as it was."

"What are your dreams like?"

"Dream Time very much not same as Earth Time. We choose what we want, where and...can not say, have not words yet. Some day I tell."

"You pick your dreams?"

"Is more. Other day I tell."

"What happens when your kind...die?"

She shrugged, waving one hand. "Bodies return to earth, we fade, are gone. It not matter. Always new life. Earth continues, life continues, male and female continue. You want I put shirt on now, Mik-ail?" She smiled, leaning over him and shooing away a nosy hummingbird. As he opened his eyes, her nipples brushed his chin....

❦

To get back to the others, it always was kind of difficult for me to figure out why Maude did what she did, or how, or how she knew when to do things. Though she tried to explain it, I could never get into that psychic stuff. Astrology and such never meant much to me, but I have to say it worked for Maude. Guess the world has a lot of strange ways. She may live mostly in her head, but she's plenty smart—not the scattered, featherbrained sort.

It was mid-afternoon the following Thursday and the summer overcast was thinning, burning off, getting pretty warm for the coast, when Maude and the others returned to the logged over slope and the old campsite. Jeb drove the colorful van off the road, parking next to the firepit. As the dust settled, Jeb turned, looking at Maude.

"All the same, Maude, 'cept for the bulldozer there." He pointed with his chin at Buck's tractor floating in a cloud of dust as it backed and turned.

Maude opened her eyes, looked at the big yellow tractor, and shook her head. "That does not feel right, that machine being here. Look about, Jeb, see what they are doing while I look into the ravine. We will make camp in the grove as soon as you are finished."

"Reckon they're after that stand of fir up the ridge."

"Perhaps."

Hensley leaned forward from the back seat. "Kin we watch the cat, Maude, or are we hidin' so's he won't see us? He makin' a road to go somewhere?"

"Likely making a road. See our van anyway." Jeb stepped out, looking about at the slope and hillside.

Maude slipped out the other side, stretching, reaching high as Clare and Hensley climbed out of the back. Jeb joined her. "Someone there, Maude. By the bushes front of the ravine."

Maude lowered her arms, frowning. "Where? Oh yes, I see him, he might be the dark man Clare mentioned in that last session. I will speak with him. See if there are any others with that tractor and what they are about."

I was chopping some brush behind Buck and saw them drive up and talk, and then Jeb walked across the slope toward us. Michael stood in the shade of the rock outcrop watching as Maude walked toward him, then he moved forward in the brook to meet her. Maude told me their conversation later.

"Not much of a place for camping here, lady, with the tractor making so much noise and everything. If you're lost, I..."

"We are not lost. We have recently been here and are returning to complete our work. I am Maude. Who are you?"

"Michael." He looked back toward the ravine, frowning, then back to Maude. "When were you here last?" Barefoot, he stepped from the brook onto a clump of dry grass, facing her.

"Last Sunday. It appears that you know about the grove beyond this ravine, is that correct?" He just looked at her frowning. "We found the redwood grove beyond this ravine last Sunday and are returning to it now."

Michael hesitated, staring at her, then at the two by the van. "You want to camp, in the grove?"

"Yes, we returned to camp in the grove. We have more to do there. I was not able to complete my studies in the grove." Maude paused, watching him, head to one side. "Or perhaps it was complete. Perhaps something happened after all." She smiled, eyes lighting.

"Sorry, I'm already camped there and I came out here away from the city for privacy. To get away from people. Perhaps some other time. You..."

"What is your business here?"

"I'm just camping out for a while, getting away from the city. You know how it is, got to get away sometimes. Sorry, but first come..."

"You are hiding something."

"Now look, I..."

Maude stood taller. "From your appearance and manner I suspect that you are a Cancerian. They do not hide things very well, though they try, and they tend to be very protective of what they have. Especially relationships. What day did you arrive here and find the grove beyond this ravine, Michael?"

"Now just a minute. I got here on Monday and the next day I found this ravine, followed it. I really do like privacy, that's what I came out here for. There are lots of other camping places around, over by the coast or up the highway by the Klamath river. State Parks or private, lots of places."

Maude sighed and turned, looking at the dust cloud around the tractor as Jeb started back toward them. "You are surely not with those road workers?"

"Hell no! I'm from the city. San Francisco. A writer. I like to backpack and I came out here for quiet. To get away from people."

"A writer on vacation from the city. Then there is no

good reason for difficulty or difference between us. We four can camp here by the old firepit, if that is necessary. If you are camping in the grove, you must be aware of what a very special place it is. Sacred, in the primitive sense of the word. We have returned for further study and ceremony. Perhaps you are even part of what is to be. For now, I ask only that we may enter to study the grove and investigate the possibility of a response to the previous ceremony. You are welcome to join, having another sensitive person would help."

"Well, I don't know...what sort of study?"

"Are you familiar with the lore of shamanism? Or Native American rituals?"

"No. I don't think much of that sort of..."

"I will show you what to do. Did the grove call you in some manner? Call you to come to it? As you were going past the area did it invite you in some fashion, to come here and find it?"

"Well, sort of, maybe. I had a crazy dream...but what does that have to do with anything. Sure it's a special place, anybody would say so. It's very beautiful. I don't want to be selfish, but, yeah, it is really special to me. Very special. Very private sort of special."

Maude tilted her head to the other side, smiling at him as Jeb joined them. "Then you are sensitive, as a Cancerian male should be, and you are hiding something. Or perhaps, someone? Is there someone else there, someone perhaps different from us? A very attractive young woman perhaps?" Michael stared at her, teeth and fists clenched. "Someone you want to protect. I have told you, we did a ceremony Sunday, a ceremony to summon someone. Did she come? Have you seen her? Ah, you are blushing. I think you have met her and she is behaving true to her kind as the legends suggest."

"Now wait a damn minute. I don't know what you're talking about. I..."

"You have no reason to hide her from us. We are her friends. I called her from her sleep Sunday night. You have spoken with her?"

Michael let out a long breath, loosing his hands. He turned back toward the ravine, then to Maude again. "I don't understand what you're saying. So I have a friend with me, a young lady. That's none of your business."

Jeb cleared his throat. "Maude, we passed this fellow near the highway when we left Monday. By hisself then."

"Ah." Maude straightened, smiling more broadly. "She did awaken. You have a 'friend,' but you did not come here with her."

"Now look here. This is..."

"This is Jeb. Jeb, this is Michael. He was just telling me about a beautiful young woman he met in the grove. Is that not so, Michael?"

"Dammit, wait. You have no right to..."

Jeb laughed, his deep voice startling Michael. "Looks like you told true, Maude. 'Bout the way of these dryads." He chuckled, watching Michael blush even more. Michael did blush real easy.

"Easy, Jeb. We do not wish to unduly embarrass you, Michael. What sort of relationship you have with your 'friend' is your own business. We only wish to meet her and speak with her. Learn from her. We can camp out here and not trouble your privacy at night."

Michael slumped, looking from one to the other, then out over the slope. "That tractor..."

Jeb nodded. "Only one fellow driving, another hardhat watching, helping. Not paying any 'tention to us."

"How do you know about who I might meet here? You...did you set up something? Damn, that's gross!" Michael straightened, clenching his fists again. "You were here and you set up something and I just walked into..."

Jeb stepped closer. "Whoa, fella. We didn't set up anything for you special. Easy there now."

"But you said you were here Sunday and...God, no!"

"Michael, please calm yourself. We did not know you existed before this hour. The ceremony we did had nothing to do with you or any specific person. I informed you, the ceremony was intended to summon a Nature Spirit, a dryad. I found an ancient Greek scroll, and, after translating it, I tried a ceremony it contained combined with some material from Native American ritual. It had nothing at all to do with you personally. I know of her kind from my studies, though I very much fear that few are left in the world. I only want to meet her, speak with her and learn about her, nothing more."

"Why do you want to meet her?"

"I study these things, shamanism, rituals, and ceremonies of primitive peoples. There is much we can learn from them. Much that our ancestors lost or left behind that might be of inestimable value in solving our present global environmental and social problems."

Michael slowly relaxed again. "I don't understand any of this. She's so different I..." He shook his head. "I will ask her if it's all right for you to come in and talk with her. She says it's her property."

"Very well, do ask her while we make camp. And please come out and tell us her answer as soon as you can. I have waited and studied for many years for this day." Maude hesitated, then turned away and started toward the van. After a moment, Jeb followed, glancing back over his shoulder with a grin. Michael pushed his way through the concealing clump of salal, back into the ravine.

Late that afternoon, Maude, Jeb, Clare, and Hensley walked into the clearing beside Weitchie's mother tree. Clare was clapping her hands and dancing about while trying to pull an open-mouthed Hensley behind her. Jeb kept shaking his head and muttering to himself, grinning like he might split his face.

"Sure has brightened up some, Maude."

"Oh, yes. It's so beautiful, isn't it just wonderfully alive, Hensley?"

Maude was as excited as she ever got, twisting a braid with her fingers as she stared about at the flowers, birds, butterflies, bushes, and smaller trees— all glowing in the low shafts of sunlight streaming through the tall trees.

Guess that for once, Maude was speechless.

Michael waited beside his yellow tent and Weitchie had been watching as they came in, seeing what they would do. They just sat on the ground or on a small log by Michael's tent, waiting and watching the squirrels and flying creatures and looking all about.

As soon as they were settled, Weitchie stepped out of a bank of the pink flowering rhodies, standing against her mother tree in the long purple flannel shirt. Michael jumped up, taking her hand.

"Weitchie, are you sure it's okay?"

"Yes, Mik-ail, all okay, I know this one." She turned to Maude, smiling. "You call me from Dream Time, call very strong. Why you do so?"

Maude stood, hesitated, staring at the small dryad, then she sat again. "It is my way to seek old knowledge that has been lost. I believe you can tell me so many things of the old ways of primitive peoples, and of how you live, and what it is like to be a part of a natural system, and...oh, so much!" Guess that was the first time Maude ever ran out of words.

Hensley finally found his voice. "Gosh, she's sexy, better'n movies. Look Clare, pointed ears. Bet she's from somewhere way far away, like Spock."

Clare giggled. "Shh, Hensley, she lives here. Always."

"Like that?"

"Of course, that's the way she is. Shh."

Weitchie smiled at Hensley. "Not glad feeling for me that some human find me so strange, but is so with many, some even have foolish fear. Do not be so, I am of the earth, same as are you. Not so different."

"Not scared, just awesome. An' what's yer name, Tinkerbell or somethin'?"

Weitchie walked closer to Hensley, holding her hand out to him. "My father what you call Indian Chief. He call me Weitchie." She turned her head, looking at Michael. "Some touch me, but still not think I am real." She turned back, laughing, taking Hensley's hand. "For you I am real, young friend?"

Hensley blushed pink as he held her hand. "Yeah! You're sure real, your hand's real warm, an' you, well...oh, man!"

"So I am." She turned to Clare. "And you, what name, who are so different on inside than out. You know me?"

"Oh, yes, Weitchie. You're real, and awesome, and beautiful. I'm Clare, and I don't understand."

"Thank you, Clare. Maybe soon you see who you are and understand much more of all things." Weitchie smiled at Jeb, moving to stand very close, looking up at his face. "You see me, man tall like my trees?"

"Aye, I surely do, miss." Jeb touched her hair lightly then dropped his hand as Weitchie turned, looking at Maude as she walked around to sit beside Michael on a half-buried root of the tree.

"What I call you, strong woman who call me from dreams?"

"Maude will do. Do you know our word, 'dryad'?"

"Oh yes, I learn many of your words."

"Will you please tell us what it is like to be a dryad?"

"I am being of forest, heart of forest. I am one with all life in forest." Weitchie's face stilled. "But where was forest is now no good life, only death. What you humans do to my forest?"

Maude hesitated. "I am truly very sorry so much of your forest is gone. How far did your personal aura of trees extend?"

"Far way, and my sisters so beyond. Now can nothing see beyond little place here. Only few more my trees left than I have fingers and toes. What is beyond? Where my sisters?"

"I do not know of any of your sisters, though I have sought them. There are many big trees still left by the coast. They are protected."

"By great water my sisters still are?"

"I think, perhaps, some may still be there, but we did not know of you or your sisters. Not with certainty. Much has been forgotten by our people. Do you talk to the trees and the animals? How do you eat? Where do you live?"

Weitchie smiled sadly. "Other human male I meet, called McEvoy, many earth turnings back, he also have much questions. I will tell you all when time is right. First, must make new forest. For that, help I need from all. Must make forest all new again, then much time for talking of all things."

"But I need to know all about you. I have waited for years to..."

Weitchie stood, looking up through the trees for a long moment. Then she looked down again at Maude sitting on the small log. "Forest must make new, with new life. Then have much time talk of all things. You help make new?"

"None of us know much about trees or forests, how they grow. I believe that science is called silvaculture." Maude stopped, looking at Jeb. He shrugged. "To replant all of the trees that have been taken, finding seedlings, people to plant them..." She shook her head, braids swinging.

Jeb cleared his throat, pulling his eyes from Weitchie. "Takes time, growing a redwood tree, lot more for a forest, some centuries. Know some Hoedads. They do that, planting trees, all kinds. Could make a start."

"Centuries! You and I do not have centuries, old friend."

"As man Jeb say, many earth turnings as human live, but not long for me. I am life of forest—how you say?—vitality? Is right word? With me, little seed have good start, grow good, when all is right. When dryad have good mate, have strong male, then all good, new tree grow fast. Only few of what you call century for new forest make. For me, not long time."

Maude glanced at Michael who only watched Weitchie, then she looked back to the small dryad. "Your life span, is it the same as your trees then?"

"Forest from earth beginning, come and go. Many dryad come and go. I have life same like mother tree. Always so for dryad, same birth, same life."

Hensley laughed, pointing at the huge mother tree. "But yer too small for being the same as a great big tree like that."

Weitchie smiled at him. "Like idea of tree, in tree's long, green dream. Idea not need be so big."

"That is fascinating, Weitchie, an idea of the forest itself. And if seeds or seedlings could be planted where the trees grew before, you could help them grow faster as long as you have a mate. Is that right? And once started, you would be here for a long time to work with them, care for them?"

"Yes, it is so."

Maude glanced at Jeb again. "That explains much about the old tales. Dryads are not just promiscuous and seductive, but must have a mate for the health and vitality of the forest." He nodded and she turned back to Weitchie. "But trees surely can live without you. It seems that many do."

Weitchie shook her head. "Not same. Not right. Live

yes, but not have same vitality, not strong, not have good long life. Tree not live good life without dryad. Baby tree not have good beginning. You understand what I say?"

"Yes, I believe I do understand. The trees are more resistant to insects, disease, or other stress when you are with them. Especially the young ones."

"Yes, it is so." Weitchie paused, eyes going unfocused for a long moment.

"Also not good thing nearby, and others, make bad noise, bad smell. Furry cousins not like. Thing there now, very bad." She pointed toward the entrance to the grove. "Must go, must no such come here. Can you make it so? Then make my forest new and have much time talk of all things."

"The tractor? I am not certain that we can stop all machines from here. That would be very difficult though I suppose we could start in some way."

"Is mine, all forest that was, even by human ways. My friend, prospector McEvoy say it so. He make it so."

"He somehow protected your forest?"

"Yes. McEvoy made it all well with human ways."

Maude shook her head. "Even if we could somehow prove you had title to this land, which may have complications, there would still be problems. You have slept for a long time?"

"What you call years, so many as fingers and toes since last I wake and love my trees. All well with forest then."

"The trees outside this narrow canyon were cut while you slept? In the last twenty years?"

"Yes. Much change, very fast. I not understand these things."

Michael rose, standing beside Weitchie. "It's hard to think about the world out there, and I don't like to say it, but my family, they have some influence. I think my mother owns stock in the timber industry and she contributes to state politicians. I can talk with her."

Jeb rose too. "Might make a start, Maude."

Clare held one long arm out toward Maude as Hensley rose, nodding.

Maude looked at them, then rose with a sigh. "So much to speak of...You have all decided so quickly?" They nodded. "I am outvoted. Let us talk about what we can do in the morning. Best for now we find our way out before full dark, make our camp, get some sleep. Thank you, Weitchie; Michael."

They parted, the four finding their way through the bushes and huge tree boles to the ravine and their van. They neither saw nor heard Frank following them in the waning moonlight, or the great horned owl gliding silently overhead.

❦

The next day was a Friday, August 11, and Buck talked while I drove him back to the shop. In those days, I always drove Buck out to the job and back to the shop yard again after work each day, helped him with the road grading or fetched things for him. Buck usually had things to say as I drove.

"Really ought to come have a beer with us, Joe-boy. Do you good after a day driving around like this, eating dust. Wash it all down and do you good. Sardi's got fine draft. All the other fellows go by after work or on weekends, if they're not mowing their lawns or something."

"You going to get the guys again this weekend?"

Buck laughed. "Those guys'll never learn. How you say it, incorrable, something like that?"

"Incorrigible."

"Yeah, that's it, that's the word. Can't learn. Not about the Forty Niners anyway. Anybody could see the Pirates didn't have a chance Monday night. Anybody at all could see that!"

"Steelers."

"Steelers, smealers, that outfit from Pittsburgh. No way they could score more than fourteen points that day. No way, Jose. It was a dumb bet. Those guys at the shop never learn."

"Don't be too hard on them. Good bunch other ways, just get carried away with football."

"True 'nough, football and beer. Anyway, only took them for fifty this time, like you said. Better not overdo it with friends. Bought 'em a round."

The light green pickup bucked like an over-aged horse throwing its head back with memories. Buck straightened his hardhat, sitting relaxed with one hand on his seat belt, the other cradling his coffee cup. "Sorry. Didn't see that one."

"No problem, Joe. I'll smooth it out with Suzy when I get to it."

"Suzy? Thought your cat's name was Adrian."

"She's changeable. All women are. Yeah, damn! I'll have to fix this part of the road for sure, Joe. Nothing but wash-out." Buck stopped to pour the last of the coffee from his big Thermos. "Yeah, this mother's son is careful. Real careful. Anyway, still forty bucks more for my Vegas stash. It's building. Building good. Soon I'll have what I need to pull one on those Vegas hustlers. You'll see this time."

"Can't beat them at their own game, Buck. Nothing good comes fast or easy."

"Ah come on, Joe, wheel this pickup back to the shop, but don't preach."

"Sorry. Fine sermon they had at the Baptist church last Sunday. Preacher had some good things to say, talking about how it was in the old days with the pioneers and prospectors. They were a hard, tough bunch. Forgot myself."

"No problem. Since when you a church-goer, Joe?"

"Not really, just like to check them out once in a while."

"What's with this McEvey business you was talking about with the guys? He one of those old prospectors or something?"

"Yes, McEvoy. A hundred years ago. Staked out a claim by where we're working, whole 160 acre homestead. San Francisco lawyer made up a fancy deed and will so it couldn't be logged or sold again or anything. Somehow, they logged it all anyway, guess nobody was watching. There might be some more trees there somewhere. Saw it on the map."

"What map?"

"That old map I showed you. Found it a while back when I was cleaning out the office attic. Got to looking at some of the stuff. Real old. Some a hundred years or more. That name just sort of popped out at me. McEvoy. Got curious and went down to Eureka and checked the old records. Maybe I'll drop by over the weekend and scout around. See if I can find his cabin or anything. Had to live here for five years and work the land to claim a homestead."

"Better you come have a beer or three with us, Joe-boy. Good for you. Being a bachelor and all, you should get out more. Why would you want to spend your weekend hiking around out here when you can tip a few at Sardi's? Forget that old stuff. Doesn't mean anything anymore."

"Haven't seen any sign of a cabin or anything yet, but there's that ravine above the road there. I might take a look up in there."

"If there're trees around, Ol' Barron will find out, one way or another. He doesn't miss much, ol' BM." As we left the logging road and turned onto the smooth black asphalt, heading south in the quiet forest Friday afternoon, Buck started singing off key. "What Barron wants, Barron gets. Yeah man!"

❦

INTERLUDE: Barron sits at his big desk, elbows on the blotter and phone tucked into one shoulder, looking out the picture window over the shallow valley that holds the mill and the small town. He leans back in his padded swivel chair, taking the phone with one hand, clicking a pen against his teeth with the other.

"Right, Josh. Yes, you understand? I'm hurting, really hurting this time....

"Sure, you know how it goes. Shirley keeps threatening to walk out on me and Marge is getting harder and harder to please. She doesn't like it, living out here in the boonies. Hell, you know her, she's your sister, wants to spend all her time in the city with department stores and the opera....

"Right. That's the way of it. You got it." He sighs, leaning forward again. "That Shirley is really something. Does pretty good working at that club, but she's got big ideas and curves to go with them, and she knows it. Damn! I gotta figure out something....

"Right. Anyway I've got to find more timber I can buy and harvest. Preferably redwood. And damned quick!...

"Right. We're cutting some down that way, but I need more. A lot more. That IRS audit's coming up and so is Marge's birthday. God!...

"Right. I'm counting on you to help with the audit. Always good to have a lawyer sitting in when those bloodsuckers come around....

"But I've got to find more logs, Josh. Got to."

"Right. Did you call Attos like I asked?...

"That bastard. After the big contribution I made to his Assembly campaign last year. No gratitude....

"Politicians are like weather cocks, turn with any

breeze that blows, but I'm telling you, they better get it together if they want any more of my money. You tell him that. Polite of course, but make sure he hears you....

"Right, that's what I hire you for, Josh, I know you're good at that. Not like me. I haven't near enough patience for dealing with those people in Sacramento. Bureaucrats or politicians....

"You're right there! We make a good team, Josh, but I have to run now. Call that old bastard and explain things to him real plain. We must have more logs. Spell it out in four letter words if you have to. Okay? No more forest tied up by these damned environmentalists. We must keep the mill running, must keep men working so they can pay taxes and support the government...and their families....

"Right. Bye Josh."

Barron replaces the receiver, staring out over the mill and the smoky town beyond for a long moment. Then he turns to the computer, punching keys and watching the glowing amber screen. After a few minutes, he stands, steps to the wall and pulls down a map, searching.

❦

3

THE CAUSE

...Trees growing wild and natural touch something in me, a place where I'm connected to nature, to the earth. Part of my nature. I understand that now, and the redwood forests are extra special for me because they're so quiet and peaceful. When I'd really awakened and walked among those great trees, I could never forget that peace. Maybe it's just because they're so big and tall, but for me it's a lot more than that.

The timber industry spends a lot of money telling people that trees are just there to be cut and milled into lumber and they say they need to harvest the "overmature" trees as fast as they can, until the trees in their tree farms are big enough for cutting. They don't talk about whether their "carefully managed tree plantations" will fill a person's deeper needs, and they make fun of the idea that trees somehow have feelings. They just don't understand. Or won't.

I used to think like the timber industry people, if I thought about things like that at all. Mostly I was just going on from day to day without really thinking. Started thinking a lot more after I met Weitchie, and a lot different. Now I can't be around those trees without feeling something special I can't find anyplace else, especially not where there are lots of people.

And Weitchie herself, earthy, exotic, some might say sexy, but for me she was quiet, peaceful, and special like her trees. Psychic ambience, Maude called it, but Maude sometimes talked over my head by a quite a bit. She has a Ph.D. in anthropology, but no one but Jeb knew that then. She liked experimenting, trying different things, and arguing her ideas; discussion she called it. Listening while she and Frank "discussed" these new ideas helped me to understand and get a lot of things straight in my own mind.

Frank is short and built square with long arms. His long black hair and full beard is kinky enough to hide his face, except for a beak of a nose and those sharp black eyes set kind of close. First time I saw him with his scuffed leather hat and dirty jeans, he reminded me of a wild man I saw in a carnival once who was supposed to bite off chicken's heads. He'd been watching everything that happened around the area without anyone knowing, until one morning he walked quietly up while Maude and Jeb were fixing breakfast beside the van. Clare and Hensley were asleep in their double bag. Buck and I were working at finishing the new road to the nearby ridge. When Maude told me about all of it the next January, the first thing she remembered was the smell of coffee and bacon in the still air as she and Jeb talked....

"Jeb, I'm afraid Michael is badly infatuated. I have never seen a man in a worse case. The old stories say dryads have that effect when they wish, and I am troubled about what he will do when she is through with him. She will apparently live much longer than we and may not really care about anything but her forest. I don't think he understands that."

"Got a point, Maude. He is sure caught up with her.

Can't see anything else at all. But he's not complaining any, seems pretty happy. Might all work out. Wonder who this feller is coming yonder? Odd looking sort." Both hands occupied, one with a frying pan and the other with a piece of jerky, Jeb pointed with his chin. Maude rose and stood beside the van, frowning, hands on hips, watching as Frank walked up. She spoke first.

"Who are you and what do you want here?"

He stood for a moment, looking around the campsite, running the fingers of one hand through his thick black beard. "Just call me George." He tipped his scuffed leather hat back and pointed to his grungy t-shirt imprinted with **HAYDUKE LIVES** in big letters. "Just hanging around the area. Got nothing better going right now and curious what you folks are up to."

Jeb smiled over his shoulder as he flipped the eggs. "Morning, George."

Maude stared at the newcomer. "We have no interest in one of your kind and would appreciate it if you would continue on your way. Immediately!"

Frank stood very still, facing her, eyebrows raised. "What's that supposed to mean, 'your kind'?"

"One of those who try to impose their minority will on others through violence and disrespect for law. Anarchists!"

"Well, shit woman, think about it for a minute. The American revolution started that way. A few men got together in a bar, tipped a few tankards of ale, raised some hell, and dumped British tea in Boston harbor. Other actions like that, too. Cost old King George and his toadies plenty, and helped them decide to leave us alone. The American revolution ain't done yet and some of us are continuing the work. Trying to wake you dinosaurs up 'fore it's too late."

"Violence always rebounds on the perpetrator. Read history yourself."

"That may be true, but strong action wakes people. Anybody sees need for change in this age of obscene consumerism, they gotta yell real loud before most folks will hear. If the dinosaurs had a few of 'my kind' they might still be around. They got too fat and too many, couldn't change when change time came around." He sighed, looking around at the stumps. "Can't you see it's just not right for any critters to get too fat—or too many? Too many of any species, the population gets reduced. Law of nature, and natural law's a lot more real than your man-made kind. That's what I'm trying to do, stop the extinction of our over-fat society—along with saving all the other critters that're dying with us and because of us."

Maude took a deep breath, staring down her nose at him. "The brontosaurus laid delicious eggs, then went off and forgot them, which was surely a consideration in her extinction. Our ancestors had some fine meals from those eggs. There were numerous other factors as well that are not pertinent today for the human race. We look after our young."

"Yeah? Been to a big city kindergarten lately?" Frank shook his head and turned, looking at the rotting stump. "Never any real change without a death or two, or a million." He turned back to her, pulling his hat off and slapping it against his leg. "What I came by for is to ask what you are up to with a woo-woo ceremony and a chickee decked out from Disneyland back in that grove."

"You spied on us!"

"I watch everything happens around here."

"Why?"

"I asked first. Why the mummery with the chickee, chanting and all?"

Maude hesitated, then sighed. "You would not believe me."

"Try me. Might be surprised."

"Breakfast ready, Maude. You like some, George? Got no more bacon or eggs, but lots of oatmeal. And coffee." Jeb held a plate out to Maude, a steaming cup of coffee to Frank.

Clare slipped out of the sleeping bag, pulling a granny dress down over her long legs. "I'll have some, Jeb. Oatmeal, please, with honey."

Maude ignored the other two, staring at Frank. "If you were there last night you saw her, George, or whoever you are." He nodded, sipping from the cup. "She is real, a dryad of the redwood forest. A Nature Spirit. We woke her with an ancient Greek ceremony."

"Okay, I've read some Greek mythology. So why the act?"

"To prove, among other things, the reality of Nature Spirits, and that there is more to the forest than just wood to be harvested."

"Shit. So you're starting some dumb nature cult? So what? If there were such a thing as a dryad like the old legends, will that help stop the killing of the forests? Where's she going when her trees are all logged and milled, or shipped out to the Far East? Anyway, how could she stand being around this lousy chain-sawing, bulldozing, 'kinder, gentler America'?"

Jeb cleared his throat. "Got a point there, Maude." Maude turned, frowning at Jeb, but he went on. "That's what she was saying last night, needs help restoring her forest. Maybe also needs help herself? Can't do it alone nowadays. Sit an' eat, eh? Clare said a dark fellow was coming, remember?"

"That's right, Maude, you told me I said that." Clare stared wide-eyed at Frank as she spooned her oatmeal.

"But not..." Maude turned back, staring at the shorter, dark man. "Very well, but you must understand that we are law-abiding and we have certain rules for anyone involved with us. No violence and you must have your chart done."

"Chart?"

"Astrological horoscope. What is your birthdate and time?" Maude turned to the open door of the van and, reaching in, opened a box, returning with an ephemeris in her hand.

Frank snorted and shook his head. "Well sure, lady. Shit. Woo-woo time already for sure. Okay, I was born on December 8, 1960. Ma said early in the morning. All I know."

"You have a birth certificate to confirm that?"

"You crazy lady? What would I be doing with a damned birth certificate? Wipe my ass?"

Maude just looked at him. "By your smell, that might be useful. Very well, I will do a solar chart for you. No, on second thought, Scorpio rising, I can see that much. And what is your name?"

"Whatever you like. Frank Godsell, it says on my driver's license."

Maude opened the ephemeris, studied a line, then stood, looking up at a pair of hawks circling over the draw. "As I suspected, Sagittarius." She turned back and studied him while he sipped coffee. "I would gladly wager that you have been in prison."

"Prison! What the hell...so all right, I've been in a goddamned stinking prison with all the hempheads, winos, and like that. They busted me last year for protesting too loud when the assholes wanted to clear-cut the whole state of Oregon. How'd you know?"

"A Sagitarian with moon in Leo and a difficult chart with few aspects and most of those quincunxial. Prison is not surprising and the worst possible milieu for a man like you. Your cynicism and negative attitude are not surprising considering."

"So I like my freedom, who doesn't? What does that 'quincunxial' business mean? Sounds like porn."

"It is a planetary aspect and it usually means that such a person tends to be unpredictable and unstable. It means that different parts of his psyche do not communicate. In other words, he never lets his right hand know what his left is doing, and friends never know what to expect of him or what sort of behavior he will indulge in. With a Leo moon, you want to be the star of the show, the center of attention, and the leader of any enterprise. And you will use unusual and eccentric means for getting that attention. Very unstable."

"Well, I'll be double dipped in chocolate-brown..."

"Possible, but unlikely. If Clare had not said someone like you would be joining us, I would not tolerate your presence beyond this moment. As it is, stay if you want, there is apparently a reason for your being here, dirty mouth and all." She turned back to the van, replacing the ephemeris.

"So, where's my chart? You going to tell me more?"

"Perhaps, some day." She stared at him as she picked up the plate of fried eggs, bacon, and toast, then turned her back, sitting on a stool.

Frank looked at her stiff back for a long moment, then jammed the scuffed leather hat on his head and turned, walking away toward the roar of the big cat pushing at a stump at the end of the road.

Two days later, Saturday, August 12, Michael woke late, half out of his sleeping bag, but reluctant to get up. He rolled over on his stomach and stuck his head out the little tent. "Why didn't you wake me, sweet?" He yawned, jaw popping. "You always wake up so much earlier than I do."

Weitchie sat nearby in the dappled morning sunshine, playing with a pair of hummingbirds and a squirrel. She turned, smiling at him. "Why should I? I have things for doing and you very tired."

"How could I be tired? Hardly did anything the last few days. Hmm. Just laid around, talked, walked a little, took a bath in the pool, brrr! Made love. But you're right, I was tired. I wonder why."

"You know weaving? Even little birds know weaving. Unweaved is word?" He shook his head. "Unraveled? You much unraveled when you come here to me. In this place you reweave yourself. Hard work, maybe for human hardest work of all. My place good for you, here where all is as should be for good life."

Michael sighed. "You somehow know, you see or sense, everything that happens in the woods around you. The trees, birds, animals, everything. Is it because you are somehow part of it all?"

"Do you not begin to feel so?" Weitchie laughed softly. "I am woods, I am spirit of this place, life of all. I am bush you pee on, so-cold water you bath in, grass and flowers and moss, or old fallen tree trunk by water you sleep on when you dream me. Does it trouble?

"No, just takes a little getting used to. Never had such colorful dreams before. Really, it feels good being so close, having you in my dreams."

"Then I am glad, for I can not be otherwise. I am made so."

Michael slid out of the little tent. Standing, he stretched. Suddenly realizing he was naked, he started to turn away. They both laughed. "I'm getting silly in my old age."

"Old habit. You forgot clothes after you, so bravely, went into the cold pool for bathing, then lie in sun. Body habits change slow, like my trees, but mind and spirit change more fast. Time have many different ways for flowing."

"Well, yeah...I guess. I better eat before we get philosophical again. Another odd thing, I haven't been eating much." He began lighting the little stove. "Which is just as well. Can't you control these pesky raccoons? Damned masked bandits are after my food every night."

"It is their way. Are you not more clever than they? You do not need so much of food now." She rose and sat beside him on the small log. "You remember, as you sleep on warm log beside pool. Did you feel me with you?"

"Feel you? You weren't there."

"I do not know word for it, for a time I feel you as part of me. Like my trees, the little water flowing, all that is in my place."

"I guess. Maybe, sort of while I was dreaming."

Weitchie laughed. "Not all dream, you see? You part of me, us, for hours, all afternoon. Where you think the afternoon go, Mik-ail? Part of you outside narrow human time flow, sometime you part of all Mother Earth. For now, you only know so in dream. One day, maybe soon, you no longer need dream for being so, knowing you, your life, be part of all. Maybe you show to other human one day. Show them to love them and my forest the same. Okay?"

"Weitchie, darling, please, no more for a while. Let me eat, and think. If you keep dropping things like that on me, I'll never get it together."

"I am sorry, Mik-ail." When Michael looked up, she was gone. He looked about, sighed, and returned to his howling little stove and his breakfast.

Michael finished his meal and stood holding the pot and spoon, watching two squirrels scurrying about, chasing each other and looking for crumbs. "Hi guys, have things changed for you too? You sure look lively."

"Yes, much change for all, Mik-ail. Much more of life for all here since you come to me."

Turning, Michael dropped his spoon. "Weitchie!" She laughed. "I'm glad you came back. You're so beautiful.

You...I..."

"Thank you, Mik-ail. Should not laugh. Even if I am so terrible that you drop spoon and stand, making a face, as if you saw something awful."

"Weitchie, you're teasing me. And fishing for compliments, but I won't give you any. Not right now. You read my mind anyway, so you know you are more beautiful than rhododendron flowers, or trillium orchids, or the hummingbirds. As beautiful as the sky, the trees, the sunrise. You just startled me."

"Did nothing, Mik-ail, just sitting here on root. And I do not, how you say, read your mind. I do not know how to read. I only see you and I know things about you. I am sorry you were startled."

"Weitchie, I can't explain, but..."

"I know, Mik-ail.

Michael pulled a shirt from his pack and sitting next to Weitchie on the half-buried buttress root, started mending, making a rough job of it. "Maybe some things shouldn't be talked about. I mean we humans, we—no, you're human too, or I'm a nature person—we are not really different, but...well, we are." She laughed at him. "How can we live together? How could we get married? How..."

She put her arms around his middle. "Think too much, Mik-ail. Also much talk. Better just live."

"Please, Weitchie, this is important to me." She pulled back as he pushed the needle through the fabric. "You can't leave this grove, can you?"

"No, Mik-ail. I cannot go beyond my trees, this small place."

"So maybe I could get a job and a place to live nearby. Maybe a cabin or something. Maybe I could even start writing—what I always wanted to do. Don't know what my family would say, but maybe that's not important now." He looked up. "Yes, maybe I can start living my own life, never thought of it that way before, always been close with the family. Mother wouldn't much like my moving out here, but what the hell, I'm thirty-six. About time. Right?" He turned to look at her, then back to the shirt. "But I'll need her help to help you get started restoring your forest. Damn!"

"Is all needing doing in one day?"

"No. But..." he took a deep breath. "I wish it could be, but yes, one thing at a time." He smiled at her. "I don't want to live without you."

"I also."

"But, still, we are different. Like how is it for you when we make love?"

Weitchie gave him a that's-a-dumb-question look, then smiled and put her arms around him again. "We are different, some ways. In what you call making love, we are some different. Always so, female and male are different. I can not say for human female, but for me, making love is always while you are here with me. When you are in my grove, you are in me. When our bodies join and you give me your male seed, it is only more than other times. Always so. While you are here in my place, I am complete and I make new life for all. Your maleness awakens new life through me. When I am fulfilled, mother tree make strong seed and all forest have more of life. More—how you say?— vitality. More of full life."

"You mean you want to have a baby? That will help your forest?"

"Not make dryad female baby now, but soon. Forest must be good first. Must be new place for her. Mother tree must first make strong new mother tree seedling for baby dryad. It is our way."

"But, would any malc do? If that's all you need to..."

"Oh no, Mik-ail! You are special. Most men not see me even little, they pass and not see. Or touch. Others only see my trees for cutting or my animals for killing.

They not see me. You see with more than eyes of body. I can not have love with one who does not wish to see me! There is more I can not explain, but I say you finding way to me and my trees was no thing of chance. If my spirit had not called you, you would not have found me. You were guided when I had need to make new my forest."

"But, do you see me as a person?"

"Of course, Mik-ail. A very male person. My lover." She nuzzled him, biting his neck lightly.

"Tell you the truth, it's still not very real for me, but what the hell? Who cares?" He dropped the shirt and picking her up, carried her to the red sleeping pad laid out on the moss, grass, and wildflowers. She unbuttoned the plaid shirt as they lay down together.

❦

Later, after bathing, Michael sat below the pool, watching the butterflies in their endless dance through the continuous mist and rainbows of the low waterfall. Weitchie was suddenly beside him, taking his hand. "Am glad you like my home place."

"It's all so beautiful, so alive, so different from anywhere else. And I keep hearing music, though I know no one is here. Like a Grieg concerto."

"Maybe is birds, falling water, wind in trees. Not know 'Grieg,' but music, yes, that I know. Not know 'city,' think it not glad place. Why you think so?"

"If I am going to help you restore your forest, I will have to go back to the city, talk to people, raise money—I don't know what all. It's depressing, thinking about it. I don't want to go back."

"Am sorry, Mik-ail. Before you come here, when you live in city, what do you care for? What make juices flow? What make you alive?"

"Well...I don't know, nothing much I guess. Until I came here, doesn't seem like I did live much. Just grew up and went through the motions, college, a job, the usual things."

"Just so, nothing of direction, nothing of purpose. No—how you say?—no intensity? Live for nothing. Better for choose something. Anything."

"What about meaning?"

Weitchie laughed. "Nothing what you call meaning. Only life. Only life."

"Now wait a minute. Meaning is..."

"Too much in thinking. You make all better if..." she paused as if listening. "Other friend come. Good we meet with them by mother tree."

"Okay, darling, but please, button your shirt. I'll ask Maude to get you more clothes as soon as she can."

Jeb leading the way, the others pushed through the screen of fern into the clearing. "Morning folks, hope you heard us coming okay." His grin broadened to match the twinkle in his eyes. "Never know fer sure if it's all right to just walk on in. Wouldn't want to interrupt anything."

Weitchie smiled mischievously back at him. "Yes, is good. Always hear you come. Always welcome you are."

Hensley whistled. "Sure is pretty here, trees sure are big. Magical. Wouldn't you like to live here, Clare? Good place to die, too."

"Oh yes, I could live here forever and forever. The trees are so awesome, such big, gentle giants, so kind and patient, and very powerful."

Maude smiled at the young couple as she sat on the log by the small fire ring Jeb had made to one side of the clearing. "Perhaps someday, friends. First we must get better acquainted and make plans. Let us sit and talk further, if that is all right with you, Weitchie."

"Yes, is good. Always be at home in my place."

"Thank you. Will you tell us more about yourself? How do you know that we are coming into your canyon each time?"

"I bet her birds tell her." Clare clapped her hands, sitting on the grass.

Weitchie laughed. "Part feathered ones, yes. My kind make talk together like our fur or feathered cousins, with bodies, not voice only. And more, for we all share same Earth Dream, same life. Many time I forget you only use words, all separate, not really know each one. I think you do not look with open heart and many time you do not hear."

"You mean that you use body language. And telepathy of some sort."

"If you call it so."

"Does your mother tree talk to you too, Weitchie?" Clare asked.

Weitchie smiled. "Oh no! Tree is other self, we feel everything same, we do not have need talk."

Maude glanced at Michael. "Your life is the same as that of your mother tree? And you live as long?"

"It is so."

"Then you think on a much longer time scale than we do, Weitchie, and yet you seem much like us in other ways."

"Sisters of tall trees, and cousins of other trees, are most long-lived of Mother Earth life. Live long, but babies few. My mother tell me of all things, as her mother tell her. We remember all from mists of beginning. We are keepers of what you call history, we live that. We are singers and dancers of great, enduring song of life of Earth and I tell you my ancestors and yours were same people. We long ago live same life."

Maude twisted a braid in one hand. "If we were the same, once, what changed? How did we come to be so different?"

"Mik-ail tell me of what you call evolution. That was a true part of way of past life, but there was much more.

Lucifer—maybe you call Prometheus—fire bringer, he divide us. You people make iron, other things from fire. With iron, make sleeping place from trees. My people not. We stay with Mother Earth same as furry cousins and birds and all other life of Earth."

Maude hesitated. "But all things are different now there are so many people. There may soon be more people than ancient trees."

"Yes. Maybe better not so many of human people. Other kinds not have place. My kind never so many. We learn find all food we need same as other life. Also we learn sleep in cold time—and dream."

"You said your dryad mother left you in the mother tree when you were born. Was your mother tree big then?"

"Yes, it is so. Mother tree give me all care, but only small tree when I am given to her by dryad mother."

"Did not your dryad mother watch over you?"

"No need. She come sometime visit in Earth Time when I am small and begin leaving tree mother, but as I grow she only visit me in Dream Time for see all is well. Now she comes not. Her trees are gone. She has not come for talk with me face to face since I last walked in forest with my first friend over hundred turnings gone. McEvoy." She smiled in reminiscence. "His time with me was very short, but sweet. Only so many turnings as I have fingers. He make homestead deed for my forest so men who take trees not come here." Her face turned serious. "Why they take so many my trees? So many gone. Must make new what has been lost, then much time for talk."

Maude hesitated again. "I've read that some redwood trees live for more than a thousand years. Isn't that right, Weitchie?"

"Many of your centuries, yes."

"A long time for us." Maude glanced at Michael who sat on the carpet of needles, leaning against the deeply furrowed bark of the mother tree and watching Weitchie.

"It would take centuries, and the government would not help, they will not pay for anything like that. Everybody knows that in these days they just plan budget period to budget period—if they truly plan at all. How can anyone think or plan thousands of years ahead?"

"I do. My trees do. It is our way. Not know your 'government,' but forest will be made new, in time. Is the way of things. Forest is destroyed many times, then comes again. Always so."

"On a different time scale perhaps. Over the millennia no doubt the forest has been destroyed by fire or ice age glaciers, perhaps many times, but that happened over hundreds of thousands of years. It is hard to know what can be done now. These times are different. Time itself is different, somehow accelerated. And many people do not like the forests, they are uncomfortable in wild places. It is hard to understand how we can accomplish this."

"There will be a way. Forest will come back. What is earth without forest? Not same. I think without forest, only death for all. Great Mother not let it be so. Redwood cover whole earth before animals or people come. First dryad make life with tree long, long, time gone. Can be so again."

Maude sighed. "I spoke with some loggers on their way to cut the trees at the end of the new road. They did not know anything about reforestation."

Jeb shook his head. "Didn't know the word."

Hensley looked up from his examination of the tiny flowers growing between the clumps of grass. "Guess cuttin' an' growin' are different, eh, Maude?"

Michael stared at Maude. "They're beginning to cut the trees there? By the new road?" he asked. He turned to Weitchie. "You knew. I'm sorry."

"Yes, Mik-ail. Not my trees, but I feel them. Not good feeling. But no sister there now. All gone. I cannot feel any sister anywhere."

"Oh Weitchie, I wish we could do something." Clare, lying on the wild grass, started to cry. Weitchie moved to the slender teenager, sitting beside her. "It may be some of you not yet hear fading screams of stumps of taken forest, but you must hear earth crying, if you will listen." Weitchie turned her head, looking at Maude. How can you not? Any of you? See, Clare does."

Clare curled on the ground beside the dryad, shuddering with quiet sobs as Weitchie held her. "Sometime this one hides her hearing for too much of pain. Peace, young Clare. We make okay, you will see, all okay soon." She held Clare until the young woman's sobs lessened. No one else had anything to say.

Michael moved restlessly, picking up a twig and stripping the bark. "We must go back to the city. That's where the information and money are." He sighed. "Got to talk to people, foresters and such. And we'd better get to it pretty soon. I sure don't want to go, but, well, winter's coming."

Hensley moved next to Clare, touching her shoulder. "I don't want to go back to the city either. It's not like here."

"Neither do I, Hensley, but perhaps we must." Clare sat up, touching his hand and wiping her eyes.

Maude shook her head. "I don't yet see how it can be done, but perhaps there is a way to restore this area. We could at least begin the process. In time we may be able to get it made into a park or some kind of protected area. Michael is right in that we need to return to the Bay Area and study what can be done." She straightened. "I will go to the university and make inquiries. You indicated that your mother has some influence, Michael?"

"Yes, I'll go and talk to her and see if she will help. Going to be a little tricky explaining, but..."

"Good." Maude stood. "And let us see if we can perhaps find others to help as well. For now, it is time we prepared our dinner back at the van." She smiled at Weitchie and Michael. "Are you prepared to return to the city tomorrow, Michael?" He nodded half-hearted. "We will speak more on these things along the way south."

Two does and a buck slowly wandered across the path as the four walked back in the afternoon stillness toward their campsite on the clearcut slope.

❦

Frank returned that evening, walking up as the others fixed dinner by the van. Clare saw him first. "Hi, Mister Frank. See, Hensley, told you he would come back. If I saw him then he has to be here."

"Guess he's back 'cause he didn't go very far." Hensley just stared.

Frank grinned at the young couple as he pushed his scuffed hat back and stood, looking at the group. "You folks really serious about restoring trees around here, protecting what's left?"

Jeb nodded. "Howdy, Frank. We sure aim to try, but none too sure of the way of it. Have some chow? Got some fine stir-fry veggies."

"No thanks, Jeb. Ate a while back. Meat. No picnic getting this land planted again. Once it's logged they just forget it. Or graze cows. What're you planning, Maude?"

Maude set her bowl down and rose, facing him. "Have you had a bath lately, fellow? Most Sagitarians like to be clean."

"No, I ain't had a bath lately, ma'am. I've been hanging out in the woods and there ain't no showers handy there. Been trying to stay out of trouble; then I go and meet you crazies. Shit! Maw always said I'd end up bad. Little did she know a bunch of nature freaks would be the end of me, even a chick dressed up as a dryad yet! Shoosh." He took the hat off and slapped it against his leg. "I like it around here and there's nothing else happening, so what are you planning? Maybe I can help some way."

"And you have no doubt been busy thinking of more violent ways to hurt loggers, or damage their equipment, trying to force them to follow your own idiosyncratic values. I've read about you Earth First!ers. Are you going to help by spiking trees or some other form of mayhem? You must understand that we can never abandon reason and dialogue, for if we do, we are truly no better than barbarians, living unbathed in the forest."

"Well shit!" he jammed the hat back on his head. "It's reasoning people make all those obscene profits from the sweat and suffering and risking of their lives of these dumb-ass loggers. And from raping our planet. You can damn well bet your long ass that everyone of them up there making the decisions have a stinking college degree. They reason real good about their profits, don't give a smelly shit about anything else." Frank turned away, took two steps, hesitated, then turned back.

"That's what I get for trying to be nice to an egghead. A lecture. Why don't you shag your long self back to whichever shit-eating university egg-factory you came from and spare us poor dumbbells your great wisdom? And we don't hurt loggers, only try to slow 'em down, so you mainstream types can 'educate' them. Never hurt anybody yet."

Jeb turned from the cookstove holding out a plate to Maude. "He shore fits Clare's description, Maude. Have some more coffee. Have a cup too, Frank?"

"Have you studied forestry, or ecology? Anything useful, Frank?"

"Some. You're not the only one wasted a lot of time in a louse-eaten university. So?"

"I suppose we must get along, for now." Maude stared at the short man. "I will never understand why the Creator has such a special interest in opinionated people.

There surely are a lot of us around these days." Maude sat down on a camp stool. "We have little experience in silvaculture or botany. Sit down with us. What do you know about these things?"

"You're sure a tough minded lady."

"Yes. How can we proceed with restoring the forest here?"

"Well I don't know that either. I've been trying to save the forest, not restore it. Took my dumb-ass degree in Medieval History. Waste of time, everything just repeats. Same old stupidities." He took a cup from Jeb. "Thanks, that's hot! First find out who owns the land around here."

"Weitchie told us that some prospector named Mc-Evoy homesteaded here and left the area protected for her. It may still be his land. Or his heir's."

"That's the dryad chick? You're still telling me she's for real? She was around when the prospectors came through here?"

"Yes. She is very real and her kind live for centuries, along with their trees. They occasionally take a lover to reproduce and renew the energy, the vitality of the forest. If one of her own kind is not available, an elf male or some other sort, she will take a human. That is almost certainly how she met this McEvoy. He was a prospector back in the last century, when she was, for her kind, a teenager. It appears that he saw what was coming and tried to give the area legal protection of some sort.

"Lady, you can't expect me to believe a line of bullshit like that."

"Suit yourself as to what you choose to believe."

Clare held a slender arm out toward the dark man. "Mister Frank, she really is real. I've touched her, she hugged me. And her ears and eyes and everything, she's not like us, but she's really real. Isn't she, Hensley?"

"Yeah, she hugged me too. Like Clare says, she's real, magical and spooky."

"She's not spooky, Hensley!"

Hensley shrugged, taking another bite of his dinner.

Frank set his cup down. "So okay, I'll go along, maybe you've got something. Nothing else has worked to stop these earth rapists. I've done some street theater, might make a good show. You loonies insist..." He stoked his beard, looking away. "First go to the county seat in Eureka. They got the files on all the land around here. See if they ever heard of your McEvoy. Homestead may be on file there, damned bureaucrats never forget anything."

Jeb held the coffee pot out. "That's right Maude, old homesteads are all recorded, if our gal's got it right. More coffee, anyone?"

Frank held his cup out. "But McEvoy might've just given her grandmother or whoever was here a line. Chickee like that, a man would promise anything."

Maude stood and laid her bowl and cup on the trestle table. "Michael will speak with his family in Atherton, I will go to Berkeley to the university for my research. What about you, Frank?"

"What every group needs, a four-star general. Okay, okay, that's sort of a compliment. I know some of the environmentalists and such around here on the North Coast. You can leave me off in Arcata and I'll talk around."

"Good. We need to know something of the local history and who has tried redwood reforestation in the past. Will you look into that?" Frank nodded. "We will start early for Eureka, we can go there together, then separate, and I will give you each my answering service number so we can keep in touch. Would you like to make a fire for the evening, Jeb?"

The tree-crowned hills in the park stood out, etched in black silhouette against a rose-gold sunset as the others finished dinner and started cleaning up while Jeb set a fire in the blackened firepit. Only Clare, watching the sunset, noticed the great horned owl glide silently by overhead.

❦

The following Monday, Buck and I helped drag out, stack, and ready for loading on the trucks, the fir logs they were cutting on that ridge to the east of the old campsite. Driving home after work we were quiet for a while, but after we had turned onto the coast highway, Buck wanted to talk, as usual.

"How's your weekend, Joe-boy? Go to church? Any pretty women there? My old man always said that's the best place to meet women."

"No, Buck, no church."

"Shoulda come with me Friday night, wouldn't hurt you to stop for a beer with the boys." Buck turned on the bench seat of the green pickup, looking at me as the truck leaned on a shallow curve of the asphalt ribbon. "Made seventy-five bucks off the boys, mostly Al." He chuckled, sipping his coffee.

"Al can't believe the Forty-Niners can ever lose, plain can't believe. Never lose, ha! If I'd pushed it, he'd of bet his next paycheck and likely the one after. A couple of beers and a close game—goes crazy. Some of the others not much better when it comes to the 'Niners. Can't figure how they get so hung up on a dumb game like football. And dumb bets! Anybody could see the 'Niners were off last night. Any mother's son at all could see that."

I concentrated on driving, shifting down as we passed three overloaded logging trucks toiling up a grade behind a slow car pulling a big housetrailer.

"Tell you, Joe, I'm gonna make it big in Vegas. That's the place. No more messing round working in the woods. Never get anywhere working for the other guy. I want mine now, not waiting for wages to go up, all of that. How much farther can everything go?"

"Seems I've heard some talk about Las Vegas before."

"Awright, don't rub it in. Made a mistake last time, paying too much attention to that sleek dealer's tits when she leaned over the table. Those folks in Vegas are sharp, don't miss a bet. They got me last time but I know what I did wrong. Won't happen again, you can bet on that." He chuckled. "Truth, I knew better then, but she was sure pretty. Got me real distracted was all. Those chicks'll do anything to win. No way they'll pull that on this fellow twice." Buck sighed and put the cup back on his big empty Thermos.

"Tell me more 'bout this McEvoy fellow, Joe. Heard somebody say he was crazy as a flea trying to rape an elephant." He chuckled as I pulled out and speeded up to pass another semi.

"Don't know the whole story, Buck, but a reporter wrote about him in a paper they had then, when Arcata was the county seat. Story said he raved and mumbled a lot as he was dying, told about a young woman he lived with for years out in the woods. Called her a dryad, that's an ancient Greek word, a kind of forest spirit. Looked it up at the library. The ancient Greeks had a lot of gods and nature spirits and such. Story in the paper said he raved about this woman, what a beauty she was, and about having a family by her. Some people went out to look, figuring she might need help, but never found anyone. Knew right where his cabin was supposed to be, had the map I showed you, but never found a woman or a cabin. Nothing. According to the story."

"Weird. Had him a woman and family, and they never found anything?"

"That's the story. Lot's of the old prospectors were pretty strange, living alone for months on end and all."

"He find any gold or anything?"

"Not that anybody knows of."

"Strange. His cabin was supposed to be right up

there by that hillside we're driving by every day? No way you'd get me believing a story like that."

"Never know."

"You read too much, Joe-boy, 'specially that fiction. Carrying books in your lunch pail! Why don't you get a woman and settle down? Have kids. Quiet sort like you, you'll live longer. Working man's gotta relax, get drunk, get a little nooky, eat good—somebody else's cooking—live a little."

"Actually, what I did Sunday was come out and look around where those people are camping. Found some redwood trees there, too. Not a whole lot of them, two dozen or so, and kind of hard to get at, but some of the biggest redwoods I've ever seen."

"Joe, you smoking something funny last couple of days? Didn't know you went for that. Or was it some of those fancy mushrooms them hippies like?"

"Not like that. The ravine we noticed above the meadow there, it leads into a grove. Must have missed it somehow when they logged around here."

"You sure? Hell, they were all over the place—when was it?—fifteen years back when they cut all this area?"

"Know what I saw, Buck."

"Huh, you see what those hippies're doing? Bet that's what you were up to, get some of that young hippie ass, right? Sure you weren't smoking with 'em?"

"No, nobody around. I just poked around until I found the way into that ravine and there they were, a whole grove of big trees. It was getting dark so I didn't go in and count the trees, but they're there."

"Can't never get a rise out of you, Joe-boy." Buck shifted on the seat, turning and looking out the window. "Wonder if ol' BM knows about them trees of yours? He'd sure be happy to find him a few more big logs for his mill."

We turned into the gate of the shop yard just at quitting time as the other men were lining up at the timeclock and the sun was drifting behind some evening clouds over the ocean. Three seagulls wheeled overhead, crying about something.

❦

INTERLUDE: Barron stands in the window of his office looking over the dusty, smoke filled valley. With a sigh, he moves away from the window and sits behind his broad steel desk. Reaching, he dials the phone and leans back in his swivel chair, one arm over his head.

"Mr. Dander, please....

"Jack? Returning your call. How's it going with you?...

"Right, I promised and you'll get them. We're getting your shipment of rough-sawn lumber ready right now. Had a problem with some tree-sitters, and an equipment breakdown slowed us for a couple of days, but your lumber is being loaded on the flatcar right now....

"I understand. Yes, of course, but...

"Right Jack. I really appreciate your patience. You are my very best and most valuable customer and...

"Certainly Jack. We...

"Yes of course. I understand that we are late with your shipment and I especially appreciate your trust, but...

"As a stockholder in our firm too, why naturally we...

"Right. I understand. Right away Jack. Immediately. Thanks Jack. Bye."

Barron pulls a hanky out of his back pocket, wiping his forehead as he sighs and turns to the amber monitor. The phone rings. "Yes, Mabel?...

"A stockholder? Oh hell, this is my day. Sure, put her through....

"Hello, this is Mr. Barron. Can I help you?...

"Yes, Mrs. Duggan....

"Right, Mrs. Duggan, I...

"Yes, Mrs. Duggan."

"That is correct. I am the principle stockholder and CEO of the mill here, but I haven't heard of any grove of redwoods in that area. I will...

"I was just going to say that I will certainly look into the matter. I can assure you I will give it my personal attention, immediately....

"Yes indeed, Mrs. Duggan, as long as your son has the correct information, and she actually owns the land there, there won't be any problems. I will look into the matter right away and take care of it. My word on it....

"Right. And thank you very much for calling. It is not every day I have the pleasure of speaking with one of our stockholders. Thank you very much, Mrs. Duggan. Bye."

Barron stands as he rings for his secretary. Stepping to a closet, he pulls out a dusty bundle of maps. As she enters, he unrolls the maps onto a work table. "This may be good news, Mabel, very good news. Help me hold these maps down. Ah, here's the one we want. McEvoy...yes by God! Here it is!"

Barron points with one finger as the two heads bend together over the faded, wrinkled map showing the land east of the park. "That canyon, how in hell's name did we miss that when we cut the rest of the area? There must be more of the big trees in there. There's got to be. Get me the shop, I'll get somebody out there to check."

❦

4

LEGALITIES

...Pretty rough country around here, but I guess the Indian tribes did all right, lots of fish in the old days. Used to get sort of melancholy wondering what it was like before roads were built or the first trees cut. Before the white man came. The whole area was once covered with forest, mostly redwoods along the coast; fir, pine, and other kinds inland. Not anymore. When I was in a place where there was real old forest, it always somehow seemed familiar to me, as if I had been there before. Like a dream I might have dreamed years ago, or a forgotten song I might have heard and can't quite remember. Maybe like the home I never had, but might once have known. It's hard, thinking the whole area might once have been like Weitchie's grove.

Maybe everything around her was so different partly because she wasn't exactly human. Not that her kind was better or worse than us, just different. I read one time about a man who had taken LSD—never tried any of that myself—but around her, it was like that man described. Sensual is likely a good word, but all the senses, not just sex. Everything more colorful, brighter, more alive with smell and sight and feeling all sort of mixed in together. Changes your way of thinking being around someone like her in a natural place like that. Sure did change my thinking, when I finally met Weitchie.

Maude tried telling me, after I'd got to know her, how Weitchie's kind had been the same as humans before history, before our ancestors learned to use fire and tools and agriculture, which her kind didn't. I didn't understand that part. Anyway, I know Weitchie saw herself as part of the forest, part of nature, not separate at all, so naturally she wanted to protect and restore the forest and everything in it. But things being the way they are, she needed a whole lot of help doing that, and what she wanted didn't fit in very well with what was going on in the real world, the human world.

When the area was first settled, there wasn't much law, like any frontier. Whoever was strongest took what he wanted. Some still think that's the right way of doing things. Let the strong and the rich do what they want.

It wasn't until a couple of weeks had passed that Maude, Michael, and the others all returned from the south where they had gone to get information and whatever else they needed. I guess they had set a date, because they all arrived back on Sunday, September 3rd. Michael was first back, but he and Weitchie had only a couple of hours together before Maude, Jeb, Clare and Hensley walked in just after noon. Frank came a little later, still pretty negative and skeptical. Jeb saw him first....

"There he is, told ya, Maude. Howdy, Frank, have some coffee."

Clare, watching the butterflies swirling around her, looked up. "Hi, Mr. Frank. I knew you would come back. You couldn't stay away."

Maude rose from the log she was sitting on beside the small firepit with a grill holding a coffee pot. "Good afternoon, Frank, I thought you might not be rejoining us."

"Well, hell, if I say I do, I do. You can forget that 'not rejoining,' I always..." he stopped, staring at Weitchie. "Chickee, you sure as hell do look real. If you're not, you ought to be. Real foxy, yip, yip, yip, yaooo!"

Hensley laughed. "That a fox or a coyote? Maybe a wolf!"

Weitchie laughed as she put down the squirrel she held and walked up to Frank, hugging him. She leaned back in his arms, eyes almost on a level. "Man Frank, who hides in my woods, you are a true man. You are loving my trees. I thank you for that."

"Aw, shucks, how could any horny male resist?" Weitchie threw her arms around his neck and kissed him on the lips. "Wow!" With one arm around her waist, he reached with the other hand, pinching her ear lightly. Still smiling, she stepped back, sitting on the root next to Michael, twining an arm with his.

Frank shook his head with a long sigh. "You gotta be the best recruiter for a cause there ever was. I'll tell you I wasn't a whole lot into this scene before, but I'm going to have to do some tall thinking now." He chuckled. "So I've been wrong a time or two, so what else's new? Yeah, I'll have a cup, Jeb. Smelled your coffee all the way down the ravine."

Jeb laughed his deep laugh. "Took us all the same, Frank, at least the menfolk. Seemed the ladies got on to her right off with no problems."

Hensley tried imitating a fox too. "Yip, yip, yip, uh, what do they do next? You know, Jeb?"

"Likely depends on the vixen, I reckon."

"Oh. That's what he yips for, the girl fox? She likes that? You part fox too, Weitchie? You like that?"

Michael looked a bit embarrassed as Jeb and Frank both laughed. Maude sat down next to Jeb and picked up a notebook. "Enough, Hensley. While you are thinking things through, Frank, I would like to return to the reports of what everyone has done and learned. We had just begun." Frank sat cross-legged on the ground, staring at Weitchie as he sipped from the ceramic mug. "We have confirmed that McEvoy did file a homestead claim on this land and I have a copy of the map and his will, which is on file. After we separated, I spoke with a local lawyer and he assured me that the will and claim are valid, so the land does belong to Weitchie. Actually, he said her descendants. I didn't try to set him straight on that. I have papers for her to sign giving me power of attorney to act for her and we have to file a plan with the California Department of Forestry; then we can replant the area. There are silvaculture nurseries where we can buy seedlings, or we can gather seeds ourselves from the nearby park and plant those. I did not learn much of use at the university for they are busy with experiments in bio-engineering and tissue culture and those lines of research do not seem far enough along to help us now. I did find some pamphlets on redwood culture practices. What have the rest of you learned?"

Michael straightened. "I'll start, if that's okay, Maude?"

"Go ahead, Michael."

"I spoke to my mother and she took care of everything. She owns stock in the timber industry, or something like that. It's all pretty complicated. Anyway she made some calls and everything is all taken care of. As long as we own the land, we can do what we want. We're all set." He turned and hugged Weitchie. "Darling, we can start replanting right away."

"One moment, Michael. We still have to file a plan and it must be approved by the proper authorities."

"Just details."

Frank snorted. "Hah! Details, shit. The local folk tell me that the local mill owner, Barron, is one of the biggest eco-rapists around. Greedy as a starving dog. In fact we used to hear about him up in Oregon. Wouldn't trust him far as I could throw that big tree. Nothing's ever that damned simple when it comes to logging, or the timber industry."

Michael turned from Weitchie. "Keep it cool, Frank. This is private land. The owner can replant if she wants to."

"Yeah? So what happened to all the trees out there?" Frank gestured toward the ravine and logging road. "And how will you explain that 'the owner' is more than a hundred years old? Never got a driver's license or filed for Social Security. If she really is what she looks to be, you can't even prove she exists. No birth certificate. You going to take her into court? Shit, they'd lock us all up in the local snake pit. And that road they just put in, you think they'll just quit using it? 'Sorry ma'am, didn't know it was private,' that's what they'll say. They don't give a smelly turd for your deeds and wills. Cut first, explain later's their way."

Maude sighed and set her cup down. "Frank, they do not need to see her birth certificate or meet her. We can take care of that. And before we left I spoke with the loggers who are cutting on the ridge, and they said they would be done with the road in about two weeks. They must be nearly finished now and we can put a gate at the edge of the property when they are gone."

Jeb cleared his throat. "Sounds right, Frank, being private and all."

Clare had been listening, her eyes getting bigger. "Mr. Frank, I know it will all work out all right. The being that speaks through me in my trances always tells truth. Always."

Hensley nodded. "Yeah, she sure does tell good stuff. All kinds of things going to happen. Good stuff and spooky stuff, too."

"Not spooky, Hensley." He grinned and shrugged.

Frank shook his head, running a finger through his beard. "Maybe, but I don't like it. There'll be a catch somewhere. You watch."

Jeb held the pot out. "More coffee? Anybody? Can't much complain, we plant more trees. Might think we'll sell to them some day. Doin' their work for 'em. Don't have to tell 'em otherwise."

Frank held his cup out. "I'm just telling you it won't be so easy. If they find out about these trees, those shitheads will find some way to foul us up."

Maude straightened. "Frank, your tendency to grandstand is overdone. Such a tendency has value in the right time and place, but that Leo moon of yours needs better integration if you truly want the personal power that comes from being the center of attention. For now, why don't you restrain yourself. Be quiet for a while and let the rest of us get on with our discussion."

"Shit. Another brown-brain psychologist."

"Without self-inquiry we are no more than animals."

Frank threw his head back, howling like a coyote, "Whaooo, yip, yip, yip!"

Hensley tried, too. "Whoaoa, yip, yip..." He broke off laughing.

Maude stared at Frank for a moment, then turned. "Did you have anything else to say, Michael?

"No, Maude. Mother thought I was kind of silly, wanting to live out here in the woods, but she guessed I would come to my senses in time. She tried to get me to tell her if there was a woman involved and what she was like." He chuckled. "I can call her again for more help if we need to. She's got some good lawyers, if we need them. It'll all work out."

Clare nodded, eyes shining. "It will all work out. I've been told so."

Guess that's what they really believed.

When a logging company finds a stand of trees they can get at, they send a man to look them over and lay out a road to haul out the logs after cutting. Easy enough cutting even huge trees with modern chainsaws, but not much use if you can't haul them out. Surveying and building a road in to the trees is most often the first step after they have looked the area over.

It was on Tuesday, September 5th, one day after my birthday, that Buck and I drove out followed by a surveyor and his helper. Later, Maude made a big thing about my being a Virgo, but it didn't mean much to me. Doesn't everybody keep track of dates and things? Anyway, it was a beautiful morning, clear and cool with a faint touch of fall in the air and the four that were camping there were eating breakfast beside the painted van when we drove up. Maude put down her plate and watched as we unloaded the surveying gear. Then, followed by Jeb and Frank, she walked down the slope toward us. It was plain she wasn't happy. The surveyor saw them coming and glanced at me, then walked forward.

Maude got in the first word. "What are you men here for?"

"Well, ma'am, they sent me out to look over the area here."

"Look where?"

"Why that ravine there. I'm told there's a stand of redwoods in there."

"What makes them think there are trees there?"

"Can't say, ma'am, just sent me out to have a look."

"Don't they know this is private property?"

The surveyor tipped his hard-hat back and scratched behind one ear as he looked around. "Didn't say anything about that to me, ma'am."

"This is private property, the whole area here, 160

acres. Homesteaded. I represent the owner and she would certainly not want any more logging or other work done here."

"Sorry, ma'am, but you'll have to take that up with the company. I'm just following orders and they said to look over the area. See, we've got the maps and I can show you the work order, all proper."

"I spoke with a lawyer in Eureka two weeks ago and this is definitely private property. I have a copy of the homestead deed and the homesteader's will in my van. Would you like to see them? I suppose that is the name of your company on the door of your van?"

"Well, if you say so, ma'am. Yeah, that's the company I work for, but they must have got permission or they wouldn't have sent me out."

"I have been talking with the owner myself the past few days, and I can assure you no such permission was given. Obviously, a mistake has been made. If you will wait, I will have our lawyer call your company and correct the matter as quickly as I can get into town."

The surveyor turned and looked at me and Buck. I just shrugged my shoulders. "Well, if you say so, ma'am. Guess we could wait a couple of days. Company likes to get along with the public."

"Good. I will drive in today and get it straightened out. Thank you."

"Okay, ma'am. A good day to you." She nodded and he turned back and started picking up equipment. We left a few minutes later. The scene behind us must have been pretty wild from what they told me later. Frank never believed anything any timber worker ever said anyway.

"Like I told you, those shit-eaters always find a way. They don't miss anything." Frank kicked the side of the stump as Maude stood beside the van, looking into the distance.

Jeb went back to eating breakfast, shaking his head.

"That's real hard news. Like to know how they found out."

"Doesn't matter a stinking paternal godshit how they found out, we've got to take action, stop the bastards quick before they start cutting road. That tractor down there's a place to begin; just take out the oil plug and it won't get far. They'll have to bring in another and we will have more time for..."

"No!" Maude stared at the shorter man. "We will not stoop to petty vandalism. This is private property. It was a mistake. As soon as we have breakfast, I will go into town and speak with that lawyer again."

"Have some more coffee, Frank. Hitting that tractor's tempting, but it would be kinda mean like, wouldn't it? And they'd know who did it."

"Morning, everybody." Michael joined them. "What's this about a lawyer? Who was that just drove away?"

"Morning, Michael. 'Fraid we got us some hard news. Have some coffee."

Maude turned to Michael. "It seems that a timber company has learned about Weitchie's grove. We just talked with a surveyor who came to look it over and lay out a road into the ravine. It is most certainly a mistake. Is Weitchie all right, Michael?"

"My God! Yeah, she's fine." Michael looked at the big yellow tractor. "They're through with those trees over there? Now they want to..."

"Yeah, the shit-fer-brains want to build another road. Right here! Bastards will end up roading the whole country. All they know how."

"But they can't. It's private property. It belongs to Weitchie."

"You are correct, Michael. We told them as much, and they left. As soon as we finish eating, I will go into town and correct the matter. Do not worry; it is only a mistake."

"But they shouldn't even know the trees are there."

"That can not be helped now. I will retain a lawyer and see to it that the road in is gated to stop any more traffic."

"Well, I better come, too. My mother's lawyer would be better than any local. More expensive. I'll come with you and call her."

"Very well, that might be useful."

"Gods, you brainwashed innocents! Mike is right that you damn well better get the best shyster lawyer your bucks can buy. Then tell him to get an injunction and sue the bastards right off. That's the only way you'll stop them once they know those trees are here. Stick it to them, hard. Right in the keister. Make them pay before they even get started. It's the only way."

Maude turned on him, fists on hips. "Frank, dammit, hold off. We will get the best lawyer we can and follow his advice. That is the end of it. We will not sabotage equipment or follow any of your other violent ideas. You hear me?"

Their eyes locked for a long moment, then Frank nodded. "Just get a real good lawyer, not one of those brown-nosed, fog-brained chiselers who represents any big business connected with timber. Which is most big business, They're all cozied up together like a nest of rattlers at breeding time. Better yet, get a lawyer who's done environmental cases; then we'll see who's right. We'll see if your precious law means anything around here. Never has before."

"Yes, we will see."

Michael shook his head again. "I'll just run in and tell Weitchie I'm going. Then I'll follow you in my car. Meet you at that restaurant in Arcata where we ate last time."

Frank rose. "I'll wait and go with you, Mike. I got some folks to talk to." Maude turned back to him, frowning. "No, I'm not going to set anything up. Not yet. I'll wait and see what your lawyer can do."

They sure had a lot of faith in lawyers.

❦

Being curious about these people I'd been seeing by the old campsite, and about the trees in that grove, I stopped by that Tuesday evening after work. Just parked my pickup and walked up into the ravine again. They had opened a path along the brook so it wasn't difficult to get in there, but like the Sunday before, I stood at the beginning of the grove not thinking about anything, dazed, until the sun slipped soundlessly below the ridge and woke me.

It sure had been a surprise, seeing those big trees when I walked through that ravine before. Never forget the way that narrow canyon opened out, full of the big trees, bushes, ferns, and flowers. Got to me every time I walked in there. Rhodies, orchids, salal, salmonberry, other kinds all blooming or with berries. All the kinds of flowers I know and more I don't. Took my breath away every time. The smell of the flowers, bird calls, butterflies and hummingbirds whirling all about in the last slanting rays of afternoon sunlight--after that I knew what they meant by mind-blowing. Maybe 'entranced' is a good word, too. Don't know why it hit me like that each time, just did, every time.

Went on up the trail into the grove of those tall trees farther than I had gone before, and as I pushed through the head-high ferns at the edge of the clearing, I stopped short, frozen. That picture of Weitchie as I first saw her hangs in my memory. Always will.

She stood, leaning one hand against the soft, deeply furrowed bark, tiny beside the biggest tree I'd ever seen. Red hair, purple flannel shirt and green pants against the dull-reddish bark of her mother tree. I just stared. There was enough daylight for seeing clear, but not much color left in anything, except for her—she glowed like a glass Christmas angel.

Michael was kneeling by the tiny firepit and didn't hear me coming over the roar of his little backpacking stove, but she knew and was looking right at me as I parted the ferns. As I stood there, frozen, she stood away from the tree, walking toward me, smiling. My knees felt like soft rubber, so help me I thought I'd fall flat on my face.

"Mik-ail, we have new friend." She didn't take her eyes off me and I could not have looked away for my life. Never felt like that before, like turned to wood—and melting. I know wood doesn't melt, but that's what I felt like.

Michael looked up with a smile, quickly replaced by a frown when he recognized me. "What do you want?"

"Mik-ail! He is friend."

"Him? He is one of the men built that road out there. Were you one of the ones going to put a road in here, too?"

Weitchie frowned. "What road, Mik-ail?"

"I'm sorry, darling, I was going to tell you about it after dinner. Oh, damn! Burned supper again. Wait until I turn the stove off." He turned back to her. "Please sit down, Weitchie darling, I'll explain everything."

"But we have guest. What are you called, guest man?"

Took me a minute finding my voice, then I wasn't very clever. Never have been much on meeting women, talking easy, and finding someone like her, here, with hummingbirds darting around her, sometimes pausing, hovering.... Felt like that myself, hovering with no ground beneath me. "Uh, I'm Joe."

She smiled again. I'd never seen anyone light up like that. Most times her face was still, until she smiled, like a sudden sunrise. When she was still she was really still, but when she talked, she moved all over. Guess that's what Maude meant by body language.

"Come, Joe, be welcome. Sit with us and it may be Mik-ail can make more of warm food for you, too."

I could see from the corner of my eye that Michael had a real pained expression. "Weitchie, you don't understand. This is one of the men that's responsible for the trees being taken. He works for the logging companies."

"Mik-ail, is true I do not understand you, but I know good human man. This Joe, he is good man. That I know."

"But...please sit, darling, I have to tell you what happened."

She looked at him, then her soft red eyes sort of went unfocused for a long minute. Michael waited until she came back and smiled again, shaking her head at him. "Is okay, Mik-ail, all my place okay. Come sit, Joe man."

I found my legs somehow, walked on into the clearing, and stumbling, finally pulled my eyes from her for a moment and looked around. A buck and three does browsed on some bushes across the small clearing, beyond Michael's little tent, stretching their necks for the leaves, paying no attention to us. Squirrels and birds were beginning to settle down in a couple of smaller trees at the edge of the clearing, chattering softly with each other over the days events. I sat on the fallen log by the little firepit, guess it was a branch must've fallen off the big tree sometime. Redwood branches are sometimes as big as another whole tree. Real hard telling my feelings as I sat there looking at her; mostly I was just numb and not feeling anything I could name.

Once I got settled, Michael sat down on a big root next to where Weitchie stood by a big tree. "Darling, when I went out to see Maude and the others this morning, this man and some others were just going away in their machines. You understand?" She nodded, watching him intently. "They had come to make a new road. Into your trees. Somehow, they found out your trees are here.

They...they want to take your trees. I'm very sorry."

She sat very still, looking at him as a tear welled and ran down her cheek, then another. "So. As man Frank has said, is not so easy making new forest."

"Yes, darling. I went in to the city with Maude this morning and called my mother and she gave me the name of her attorney and I called him and he told me about another who handles this kind of case. Anyway, Maude is still in town talking with him and we'll work it all out. You don't have to worry."

"What is, 'attorney'?"

"That's a man or woman, a lawyer, who protects others' property and things like that. That's the way we do things nowadays."

"So will be okay. Why are you angry with this Joe man?"

"He is one of the ones that would take the trees, if he could."

She looked at me. "You not take my trees, Joe?"

"Uh, no. I just help make roads."

"He makes roads for the ones who take the trees. They can't take the trees without roads to get to them."

Weitchie looked from one to the other of us. "Joe not take trees. I know he love trees. Maybe he not know so, but I do. I know. Is right, Joe?"

I was just beginning to feel half-way normal and real again, but as she said that and looked at me, I was hollow. Couldn't breathe.

Guess she understood somehow, because she smiled, a twinkle in her eyes with the tears. "Human man not know what he is, what he want. Many time I see it so." She continued looking at me, so I figured I should answer somehow.

"Yeah, I guess...that's likely true."

She laughed, wiping her eyes, and Michael looked at me, still not liking what he saw. "See, Mik-ail, Joe is good man. He will not take my trees."

"I don't understand, Miss. Do you own this land, these trees?"

"I am Weitchie, not 'Miss'. I do not 'own' as your kind say, but trees and all here are part of me and I am part of all here. I am dryad, you would say, Spirit of Redwood." She laughed. "More than 'spirit,' also female person."

I sure didn't know what to say to that. Tongue-tied anyway, but I didn't want her to stop, so I mumbled some questions, and she told me a lot about herself and her trees. The same as she had told Maude and the others. Sure didn't make any sense to me then.

A while later it was plain I was a third wheel, so I got up to go. She came over and hugged me, gave me a quick kiss on the lips. Knocked the pins out from under me again. I managed to say something or other, and my legs found the way through the ferns and down the steep trail toward the mouth of the ravine. Michael came along as far as the last tree of the grove. Guess he wanted to be sure I left. "Sure you can find your way, Joe?

"Sure, I know the area pretty good. Moon's full tonight."

Michael leaned one hand against the furrowed bark of the redwood tree. "Okay. Have a good night, fella."

"Sure, Michael. See you." I pushed through the clump of salal, jumped the brook, and walked out. When I got to my truck, I just stood leaning against it in the moonlight, mind blank. Finally got in and went on to my apartment.

Maude told me later how, when Michael got back to the clearing, he found Weitchie standing against the bole of her mother tree, head against the soft, furrowed bark and face turned up to the full moon showing between the tree tops to the east. As he entered the clearing, he stopped, looking at her.

"Weitchie. You're so beautiful. Are you all right?"

"Yes, Mik-ail much all right. So lovely the moon, let us a bath take, of the moon's heart-swelling light. Maybe soon time for new baby dryad making."

"Uh, sure...oh damn, Weitchie. I can't go on like this."

She turned her head, looking at him. "What is amiss with you, Mik-ail?"

"That Joe, the way he looked at you. He couldn't stop. Stared like he'd never seen an attractive woman before. Bad enough with that disreputable Frank watching you out of the sides of his eyes—I never know what he's thinking—and Jeb, and that silly Hensley. Why does Maude let him hang around anyway?"

Weitchie stood away from the tree, her body glowing softly in the light where it wasn't covered by the dark, open shirt. "Am not knowing why Maude like Hensley, but maybe she have mother need little bit twisted. Frank much troubled but he good man; he help us. Maybe he need good woman, make him more soft, then much help, clever. Joe help too, you will see. A much good connection is made with Joe. Like roots of trees we all touch underground. Is much right we meet him for he will have a part in what is to be. I feel right with Joe. A good man, when he wakes. Maybe he wake soon."

"Yes, but, well, he's just a guy works around here, not very bright. It's not him or the others so much, but, I mean—now the timber people know about these trees, pretty soon everybody will know you're here. Frank will use the loggers knowing about the trees to bring a lot of rube backwoods 'eco-activist' friends of his from around the area. Probably all young men with long hair and beards. They'll be hanging around, and you don't even have proper clothes and you hardly keep the ones you have zipped or buttoned up. Anyway those clothes don't hide much. God! What am I going to do? I know you don't care, you're a...a force of nature. Can't help liking men.

Or they you. You're damned attractive to any man. You..."

"Mik-ail! Not understand what you say. What is matter with you?"

"All those men coming around and...well, I'm still young, too. It's just that you're so attractive. I wanted to make love to you the first moment I saw you standing on the log by the pool, and I'm not like that. I'm a civilized man. I respect a woman and, if she is attractive, I want to get to know her, sure, but not throw her on the ground the first minute I lay eyes on her. I never met a woman made me hot so fast. I know it's stupid, but you, oh hell." Michael threw himself down on the sleeping pad, black in the moonlight. "It's not your fault, but if you just had more clothes, and if you were more careful with the ones you have. And the way you move, and...oh, damn!"

Weitchie moved to kneel beside him on the pad. "Mik-ail, I am as I am. I tell you I am dryad. I need only one man for a time. You I choose, no more. Why you have trouble with this? Very much thing of nature, man and woman. You know so. Only one man I need, other connection with other man for helping make forest new and strong again. They give help for my forest."

"I know, you're not like other women. Like regular...I mean, the women I've met before. I never felt this way about any of them." Weitchie laughed, laying beside him and putting one arm around his neck.

Michael turned, half above her, placing a hand on each side of her face. "Yes, you've told me, I know you're different and I'm glad you only need one man and...I'm sorry." He swallowed. "I've never felt like this before, but I'm glad it's me. Don't have the foggiest notion how this is all going to end. God," he chuckled, shaking his head. "If my family saw me now. Weitchie, I love you. It's crazy, but we'll rebuild your forest and you and I will make a baby dryad for the future and...I love you so much." He rolled and stretched out on the pad, pulling her on top.

The moon rose higher through the treetops, lighting the whole of the clearing and the two figures moving in rhythm together on the little sleeping pad.

❦

Seems Maude had found a better lawyer, one that really knew what he was doing, and they got an injunction to stop work until ownership of the homestead could be settled. Don't know much about the sort of thing lawyers do, but I do know the way things go around here.

It was the middle of a sunny Thursday morning with a few fuzzy high clouds like gray brush strokes against the cobalt blue of the sky when Maude and Jeb got back. Frank and Michael were waiting by the old campsite with Clare and Hensley. Hensley was first to speak. "Hey Maude, we been waiting so long, thought you wasn't coming. Maybe going the other way."

"What took so long, Maude?"

"Eureka is not much of a town to spend time in. Gave me the image of a somnolent dragon, one that may never wake up, and court proceedings always take time. We started a suit to assure the possession of the land and received an injunction to stop any sort of work here, so all is well. It is good to be back. Is everything well here?"

Hensley laughed. "Yeah, Maude, except Frank's restless. He just sits still, but his eyes move all the time."

"Restless? I'm just waiting for the ax to fall, and I'm about out of beer."

"I can assure you that everything is settled and we can get on with the new planting. While we were waiting, Jeb and I met with a silvaculture grower and received some prices. We also talked on the phone with some planters, Hoedads they call themselves, pleasant people, willing to work as soon as we arrange the financing. We have not yet addressed that issue."

Frank grimaced and turned to climb to the top of the

huge stump where he sat, frowning, looking out over the slope with his leather hat pulled low.

Michael hunkered down beside the fire pit, stirring the coals. "Yes, money. Well, I can help some. When I was in the Bay Area I arranged to sell some stock and moved some money around. I can put in five thousand for starters, more later."

"Thank you, Michael, I made arrangements for applying for a grant that will help us later, and I....

Frank jumped back down off the stump, slapping his hat against his leg. "Your shit-eating later is here now! There they come again, that same mother-loving crew that was here the other day."

"Frank, please restrain yourself." They all turned to watch as Buck and I drove up, followed by the surveyor and his helper. Soon as we stopped, Buck went right down and started checking over his tractor, getting it ready.

Maude opened her van and pulled a folder out, then joined the others and they all walked down to where we were unloading the equipment from the pickups.

"Is there some problem, men? This is private property as you well know. Or have you come to remove the tractor?"

"No, ma'am." The surveyor spoke up. "Seems there wasn't any mistake after all. We're to put a road in here, into that ravine."

"It would appear that communication in your company is very poor. We obtained an injunction yesterday, preventing any work on this land until ownership of the homestead can be settled and brought up to date. I have the papers." She opened the folder and held them out.

The surveyor took the papers from her and flipped through them. "Does look like the right papers all right, ma'am."

"Good. Then we would appreciate it if you would

remove the tractor and go on about your business."

"Not that easy, ma'am. The company president told me there might be some such papers issued, but he said to go ahead and he'd get it all straightened out later. So if you will excuse me, I'll set up to start running line here."

"Now just one moment, these papers have all the proper court stamps on them. Are you just going to ignore the law?"

"Well, ma'am, there's law and there's law. I'm just going about my job." He turned away and started leveling the transit. The helper was already going up the slope with his stick. As Maude stood, for a moment speechless, the surveyor started signaling his helper to move a little left and further up slope. I stood by the pickup watching, holding more stakes and a hatchet.

"Jeb, start up the van. We will drive to the nearest phone and find out who enforces the law around here."

Frank laughed. "Right on, Maude, now you're on track. Call the Sheriff's Office, they take care of things out here in the boonies. Tell 'em to shag their fat asses out here quick. But if you want them here anytime soon, make it sound like the Ruskies have invaded and a thousand women are getting raped."

The surveyor straightened, taking two steps toward them, one hand raised, glaring at Frank. "Now wait a minute, ma'am. The Sheriff's Office gets real upset if they get called out for nothing. They could even issue a citation for a false or frivolous call. You better think twice before you go running off to the nearest phone. Could be expensive for you."

Maude straightened to her full height as Jeb stepped up beside her. "If you persist in going on with your illegal activities, you leave me no option."

The surveyor paused, looking at them. "Well, all right. If you insist on making trouble for yourselves, go right ahead. It won't make a bit of difference." He turned back to his instrument, waving the helper on.

"Come, Jeb." Maude and Jeb walked to the van, climbing in and starting up. As they backed around to drive out to the highway, Buck started up his cat, a column of black smoke rising straight in the still air. I couldn't think, just stood, looking from one to the other.

As the van started forward, the surveyor put his fingers in his lips and blew a shrill whistle, then raised both hands over his head, waving. Buck turned the big dozer, backing around, then stopped again. The van stopped, backed up near the surveyor. He walked to them and stooped, looking in the driver's window. "Look, folks. I don't want you should get into trouble with the Sheriff's deputies. Frankly, they won't be too happy with me for this either, and I got to live with them guys. So look, we'll leave for today and give you folks a chance to think things over. Maybe go talk to a good lawyer. You should get yourselves a local one; he'd know more about the way we do things. Have him call the company, and they'll straighten everything out. But you got to realize those logs are very valuable. I'm sure you can work out a good price with the company, but get a good local lawyer. I happen to have the card of one right here. Call this man and he'll help you make the best deal."

Jeb took the card, shut the motor off, and turned, looking at Maude. Buck sat still on the tractor seat, hands on the levers, watching.

Maude took the card from Jeb and got out of the van, walking around to face the surveyor. She looked at him for a long moment. "Leave. Now. I will return to town and your company will certainly hear from my lawyer as soon as possible. Now leave."

The surveyor tipped his hardhat back, scratching behind one ear. "Well, okay, ma'am. We'll leave, but you got to understand..."

"Now! Leave immediately. I will say no more."

"Yes, ma'am." He gestured to his helper then turned and waved at Buck who shut the machine off again. It was suddenly very quiet.

Frank told me later, when we had time to sit down and have a few beers together, how he couldn't sleep that night. Had his little camouflage tent set up in the shade of some bushes growing below the hillside, but the moon, which was only just past full, was real bright. He tossed and turned for a while, then got up and took a leak on a bush and got a can of beer out of the brook.

Finishing the beer, he walked down to the tractor and started looking at the tool box on one side to see if it was locked. It wasn't. He was just climbing down off the track with a wrench in his hand when he saw the headlights of an oncoming vehicle waving crazily overhead. Tossing the wrench back toward the toolbox he ran all out for the nearest brush.

The boss sent Buck and me to another job that morning, and the next day, Friday, driving back to town after work, Buck was in a good mood.

"Shoulda come with me last night, Joe-boy. Good for you to stop for a beer or three with the boys." Buck turned in the narrow pickup seat to look at me, grinning, sipping his coffee. I just shook my head.

"Be better for you, you buy some property, settle down. Good buys around Eureka, Arcata, or Crescent City. The area's gonna grow. This place we're working now, there's good property there, bordering on government land. Real good investment for a quiet single fellow with no responsibilities."

"Not for me, Buck."

"You have to admit it's pretty country, Joe, real peaceful driving along through these old groves. When I make mine and buy that condo party pad in Frisco, I'll come up here now and then. Yeah, I'll do that."

The tires squealed as I turned onto the paved highway. "Easy does it, Joe, no special hurry. You got a heavy date or something? That gal down at Sardi's? She's got her eye on you. Been holding out on me?"

"Just thinking, Buck. Summer's almost past already."

"Yeah, sure is dry still. Gonna be a dry year. Won't do the forest any good. Those Doug fir we cut that road into didn't look too good to me."

"Maybe the weather's changing like they say."

"Maybe. See odd things sometimes. Saw one of those pink rhodies blooming where I was cutting road this morning. One of the wild ones. Right alongside my Daisy when I stopped for lunch and started climbing down off the track. Real late, but pretty. Pushed it aside to get down. So tell me what you're thinking about so hard, if it ain't some woman."

"Nothing much."

"Come on, Joe, I can tell you got something on your mind. Spill it out."

"Well, last night I went back to that grove I told you about, above where we were working. There was a young woman lives there. She's real different, and I guess she owns those trees, maybe the whole homestead."

I tried telling him about Weitchie and her grove. He nearly laughed himself sick.

"Joey, Joey, you've blown it. Finally meet a woman that gets to you and you flip out. Completely. Clear off your ever-loving rocker." He went back to laughing, beating one hand on his leg, but finally ran out and still chuckling, took a last swallow from his big Thermos.

"A red head! Dressed in a purple flannel shirt and bright green slacks. Got to hand it to ya, you go for the best when you go, and when it comes to imagination you're sure the greatest. Never thought it of you, but not real surprised. Birds and butterflies and rhodies blooming—in September. Knew there was more than you showed, anybody could see that, but never thought you'd fall that way. Comes from reading too much and being horny for too many years, I guess. Yeah, must be it. Or smoking some funny weed with them hippies. That it? She a hippie? Did you get a little already? Last night?"

"No, Buck, not like that. She has a boyfriend there with her. Some city fellow, you know; we saw him a while back, the fellow with the big blue pack."

"Don't let that slow you, Joe, city fellow will be gone in a week or two. Winter coming and he'll not stick around. Your woman got her a cabin back in there in those big trees? Place you could hang out through the rainy season?"

"Not like that. Don't know where she lives in there."

"Not so good then. He maybe brought her out here. I remember he was alone when we first saw him. You're gonna have to act fast, Joe-boy, before he takes her away. Hey, she musta brought that fancy red sports car been parked by the road the last few days. Rich! You'd better move fast for sure, Joe; one like that won't keep. Give her that logger, he-man line, and don't take no for an answer. They never mean it anyway."

"I likely won't talk with her again. Like you say the rainy season could start any time. They'll be gone then."

"You say she owns that grove of redwoods. They belong to her?"

"Yes, I guess they do."

"Must be really rich, maybe too rich a pudding for a country boy, but you sure ought to give it a try. Been trying to tell you, Joe-boy, won't ever get any, you don't go after it. See something you like, go for it!"

"Not like that, Buck."

"Anyway, ol' BM knows those trees are there now, so

she won't have 'em for long. No way. Barron'll be drooling over 'em, getting ready to cut any day."

"This time might be different. That grove is not like any other I've ever seen. Maybe Mr. Barron and his loggers won't get this one. Sure hope not."

"You're just infatuated, Joe. Make out with your chickee if you can, but don't get involved in trying to save any redwoods. That would mess you up good around here. Just take it easy, go for the women, leave the trees alone."

"We'll see, Buck."

The sun had settled behind some clouds to the west over the ocean and it was getting dark as we pulled into the shop yard.

INTERLUDE: Barron is on the phone in his high-tech office, leaning back in his swivel chair with one arm crooked over his thinning hair.

"Forester Smith's office, please. Hi John, Barron. How are you?...

"I heard about that, but no problem, we'll work it out. Take care of it right away....

"Yes, the boys are getting out the last of that fir off 101 past the park. No problems there either. All a-okay....

"Right. Say, did you get a call from a Mrs. Duggan down in the Bay Area. About some homesteaded property close to that fir we're harvesting? Some old prospector named McEvoy?...

"Right. She told me the same. She's a stockholder so I told her I'd look into the matter very carefully." He chuckles.

"You told her the same. Good. What do you know about that property? Any big trees left out there?...

"You don't know of any. Okay. Listen, I found an old map here at the office. Got to looking around after she called and sure enough this old map shows a homestead off 101 near the park that was somehow missed on the newer maps we usually use. I guess someone made a mistake in copying. That road the boys just extended to that stand of Doug fir goes right through the property and the map shows a canyon there that may have been missed. You won't mind I send the boys out to look at it will you?...

"I checked, doesn't show up on the air photos of the area. If it's a narrow canyon the tops of the trees would look the same as the small, stunted trees on the ridges. You know photos can fool you in that rough country....

"Good, good. I'll look into it and if there are trees there, I'll file a harvest plan by the book. You know I spoke with Assemblyman Attos last time I was down in Sacramento, told him what a good job you and your men were doing. He was glad to hear it. Legislators mostly just get complaints. You know how it is. He was pleased to hear a compliment....

"Right, John. Glad to do it, only the truth. I told him we have our problems up here, but getting along with the CDF is not one of them. Thanks a lot. See you around." Barron lay the phone back in its cradle, a thoughtful look on his face as he dials again.

"Hi Josh. I have some work for you....

"Right. Got a call from a Mrs. Duggan down in Atherton about an old homestead up near the park. I found an old map that shows it, too. Sent a man out to look and there are trees there. Looks like they somehow got missed when the area was logged. I want you to find out if there are any heirs to this McEvoy that filed the claim. Might have done a mining claim too....

"Right, check it out. If no one has occupied the land for a long time, we can do what we want, but I want to make it look right. I spoke with the CDF and they don't know anything about it. If we can find some heirs or somebody says they are...

"Right. You've got it. Check it out for me, okay?...

"Go to it, Josh." Barron grins as he hangs up and dials the shop.

5

ETHICS

...Something in me needs a wild forest. If all my ancestors lived in or near the forest, and they did near as I can tell, then I better think two, three times before I try living differently. Seems a lot of people are content with nothing around them but concrete, plastic, or glass; some of them maybe because they've never known any different, but I couldn't live like that. Just the way I am. Can't grow roots in concrete.

Guess most men figure they've got to have a job and live wherever they can find one. A job somebody else makes for them. Not too many think about making their own job.

Some of the men I used to work with felt bad about all the clearcutting and destruction, but jobs were more important to them than feelings. Almost like jobs were somehow sacred. Now all the wild forest is nearly gone and a few are beginning to see things different, looking for other kinds of work. Not just jobs, but work. Seems that for a lot of men, your job is who you are, and if you want to change what you do for a "living", you first have to change yourself. Not easy for most of us. I'll tell you later, about my new "job".

This area was still wild and forested not long ago, and law enforcement was pretty loose. Some still think they can do anything they want, and it's hard to blame them when they get away with it. But times are changing, especially with the new environmental laws. These laws are pretty complicated, and Congress gives mixed signals more often than not, so local law enforcers often don't really know what's right. When push comes to shove, they usually go with whoever pushes hardest and that's usually the mill owners and timber industry people, the ones with the money. Like water, police and other public people most often take the easiest way. Just human nature. Hard to blame them.

The next morning, Saturday, was very still. The sky was overcast to the west with streaks of gray painted on gray like there might be a storm coming. A trio of buzzards circled effortlessly, almost without motion, spread out high in the gray sky over the draw below the stump dotted slope, as if they were waiting for something. Maude, Jeb and the others, including Frank, were fixing breakfast by the van when a County Sheriff's patrol car drove up and parked nearby. Two deputies got out and one started up the slope toward them, extra pounds straining his uniform. The other, the driver, stood leaning on the car, watching over its roof. Maude rose, put her plate and cup down, and walked a few steps forward, pausing beside the van....

"Can I do something for you, officer?"

"Might be, ma'am." The deputy stopped a few steps back. "You folks been camping here long?"

"A few days."

"May I see some identification from each of you?"

Maude hesitated a moment, looking about, then at the deputy. "Certainly, officer, I'll get mine from the van." As Maude opened the van for her big purse the other three searched for their wallets. They all showed their drivers' licenses to the deputy who started writing on a note pad.

"Dr. Madeline Kingsly, Jebediah McCoy, Clare Clark, Hensley Tod-Barton. All from Berkeley, California. None related? No. Who has registration on the van?" Maude showed him. "And this—what is it?—sports car here?"

"That belongs to Michael Duggan. He is a friend and camped nearby."

"Here he comes now, Maude. Care for a cup of coffee, Lieutenant?" The sergeant shook his head as he watched Michael walk up.

"This officer needs ID and car registration from you, Michael."

"Oh? Okay, I'll get it."

"Ma'am, what about the other man I saw leaving as we drove up? Shorter fellow, dark, with a brown hat."

Maude turned from putting her purse in the van and faced the deputy, one hand toying with one of her long braids. "Just a hiker that stopped by to speak with us for a minute. He went on."

"We didn't see any other cars as we drove in and he didn't have a pack."

"Perhaps he left his pack elsewhere. We don't know him." Maude grimaced.

"Didn't give his name, or say where he was headed?"

"No, he did not. What is the problem, officer?"

The deputy stopped to inspect Michael's papers, writing on his notepad, then turned back to Maude. "That equipment parked yonder, the watchman checks it from time to time. Said he saw someone run away as he drove up last night. Some of the equipment had been tampered with, no harm done, but looked like somebody was trying. Had some trouble in recent years with that kind of petty vandalism. Got strict laws with heavy penalties protecting workers' property. We enforce those laws. You see anyone around looks suspicious, you warn them. Fines and jail time for anyone we catch. Anybody tries to interfere with lawful workers or their equipment, doesn't matter who they are, ma'am, Dr. Kinsley, we enforce the law real strict around here."

Maude stiffened. "Are you threatening me, officer?"

"No, ma'am. Just thought you'd want to know. Good day." He turned and walked back to the patrol car, climbing awkwardly in with the notepad still in one hand. The other deputy got in, started the car and drove slowly off east toward the end of the new dirt logging road. The group went silently back to their breakfast until the patrol car passed toward the highway.

Hensley laughed. "What's he mad at us fer, Maude? He happier when he's mad? That kind's sorta spooky."

Clare shook her head. "Not spooky, Hensley, just doing his job."

Maude set her cup down hard. "Damned little trouble-making idiot."

"Ah now, Maude, have some more coffee. Frank's all right. He maybe gets a little bit carried away at times, but deputy said there's no harm done. Here he comes anyway."

Maude stood again, hands on hips, as Frank walked up and retrieved his plate from under the van. "You know why that deputy was here, Frank?"

"I can guess, but they have nothing to go on."

"So why did you hide?"

"You know I did time a few months back—you and your damned astrology bullshit—they would've taken me in and made a big-ass fuss. That's the way it is once they get your number. Hell, they stopped and hassled me twice walking along the highway. Just don't like my looks."

"So you create trouble for all of us. I want you to know that was the very first time since I was a freshman in college that I have deliberately lied for anyone. The first time in over twenty years!"

"Gee, thanks. Got more coffee, Jeb? Umm, that's

good."

"You violent, inept idiot. Besides damaging my reputation, you could ruin everything we are doing here. Can you see that? That deputy is suspicious; he will remember us. Better had that watchman caught you last night."

"Ah now, shit. You want me back in the dump with the drunks, hopheads and all? I'm on parole. Those creeps can pull me in and put me away for anything they like, anytime they like. Judge will take their word before mine any day; they're all buddy-buddy out here in the boonies. And that fat deputy is mean. I can tell. He's big and ugly enough, he can take his favorite teddy bear anywhere he wants. And I'll bet he likes busting people. I'd be lucky if all I got was jail time and not a busted head along with it."

"Have you considered that perhaps some people like being 'busted.' If they did not, they would not indulge in such juvenile, destructive behavior. If you do not find a better way to express your inner rage, or find out what lies behind it, you will always be in trouble. And your friends, if any, with you."

Jeb touched her arm. "More coffee, toast, Maude? Got plenty."

Frank held his cup out again while watching Maude under the brim of his hat. "Go on, let's hear the whole damned lecture. I can see it coming."

Maude hesitated, then sat down on the camp stool, holding the cup in her lap in both hands and looking at the three buzzards circling high over the draw. "No one has the right to harm others out of their own frustrations. Before we take any action, we must carefully assess the situation to insure that we are not projecting our own frustrations and anger.

"Ah shit, pop psychology on the menu today. All beware!" Frank sighed, tipping his hat back. "So you said it before, I hate being locked up. You got that part right. And what about insane assholes trying to destroy our spaceship we're all traveling on through this crazy universe. That's what it's all about. Picking the planet apart to get its valuables out, blowing it up, or destroying it some other way, like taking all the big trees. They gotta be stopped. One way is trashing their earth-raping equipment, make them pay for their destruction. Change the bottom line. That's all I'm about. Trying to stop the rape that fat cop is protecting. Do you hear me?"

"I understand your desire for freedom and with your planetary alignment such desire may well be compulsive, but does that give you the right to harm others? We have laws for protecting the planet, and the right to appeal those laws. That deputy might make a mistake at times, but, as you very well know, two wrongs do not make a right."

"So I've heard, but I tell you all life must be free, not just me. Everything. If everything isn't free, nothing is free and no one is fully alive. This obscene techno-industrial machine we've got is a killing machine. Killing for dirty profits for the privileged few who waste their filthy wealth trying to find some satisfaction in life or paying off the medics. They're killing themselves along with the whole world. Tell me I'm wrong."

"Yeah, tell 'em Frank, let 'em know they can't live while killing themselves!" Hensley waved his cup in the air, coffee flying.

"Hensley! Stop that. You're spilling coffee on me."

Maude looked at Hensley for a long moment until the young fellow turned away. "I do not say you are entirely wrong, Frank. there are inequities, but that is not my point. If you, because of your chosen and self-accepted viewpoint on life and society, fear of imprisonment, or whatever troubles you, resort to violence, you are no better than those you oppose. You cannot be effective in anything you may wish to accomplish if your actions spring from anger, rage, or fear."

"So all right. The two of us can sit here and spout this abstract bullwhacky till the cows come home, but what good is it? People been saying fine things, making up big words, passing laws, and preaching sermons for years. And all for what? This verbal diarrhea going to grow new trees, or save the few old ones that are left? Hell no, it ain't. We need action."

"I can see that our views remain irreconcilable. Just promise me that you will not engage in illegal activities while you are with us or in this area."

Frank put his cup down and stood. "I'll give you this: get your big city lawyer and, if he can stop the rapists, good enough. As long as they don't start cutting the trees in the grove, I promise. But if your lawyer fails, then I'll do whatever I have to do. I'm in this all the way now. Okay? That's final."

Maude nodded. "That is all I ask. We can accomplish our ends within the system. We have the injunction; the suit is under way; it will all work out."

"Lady, I hope you are right. I really do hope so."

Seems Maude and Frank could never agree on much of anything in those days.

❦

That same Saturday, late in the afternoon, I went by hoping to find out more about Weitchie and whatever was going on. Had some sort of thought of helping her if I could. Didn't see anyone, but their cars were there, so I walked on through the narrow ravine into the grove. They were all sitting around a little fire that popped and hissed in the stone-ringed firepit, talking with Weitchie and each other. A squirrel was sitting on top of the little yellow tent, eating something from his paws. As I stepped through the hedge of fern she was standing by the biggest tree looking at me, like always.

"Hi, man Joe."

"Hi, uh, everybody." She came over and took my hand. "Welcome, Joe. Joe is friend same as all here. Come sit with us." She pulled on my hand. I was doing all right, only half distracted by the grove, until she touched me, then I couldn't breathe. Somehow my legs carried me after her to the edge of the circle. The others stared as I sat down cross-legged on the grass. Guess I wasn't very welcome, but I hardly noticed.

Michael still looked pained. "Hi, Joe. Maude, Jeb, Clare, Hensley, Frank, this is Joe. He came by the other night when you were gone. Weitchie liked him, though I don't understand why."

Maude stared at me. "You were with that surveyor."

"Yes ma'am, work for a road contractor, do roads all around the area."

Maude turned to Weitchie, frowning. "This man is one of the workers who helps take the trees in the area. How can you be sure he is a friend?"

Michael nodded as he sat on the root. "Tried telling her the same thing."

Hensley moved away from me. "Yeah, Maude, he's a man wears a hardhat who makes roads that don't go anywhere to get trees."

Jeb chuckled. "Not wearing his hat now, Hensley. Not that I can see. Have a cup of hot chocolate, Joe?" I nodded and Jeb reached for a pan by the fire.

Weitchie had moved back by the big tree, close to Michael. "Maude, you say to me about what you call astrology how you know things you can not see with eyes of body. I can not explain, but I have different way; I just know. Not need reading or other things you use, only know. Always so with my kind. I think also you not need such things; only with such help you see more. I know

Joe is good man. He wants to help me and my trees. Is it not so, Joe?"

"Uh, sure. Yes, I would like to help, any way I can."

Maude looked kind of skeptical. "Do you know what they are planning to do next, or have we convinced them to leave us alone?"

"I'm sorry, but I don't know that. Sometimes we get rumors about what the bosses are going to do, or the mill owners, but that takes a while. I don't know anything about this timber sale right now.

"Well, the lawyer can't do anything until Monday, but then he will find out why you people wanted to look around here last Thursday."

"I'm real sorry I can't help more. I just work for the contractor."

"Joe will find a way for help. Tell more of what you call 'ethic,' Maude."

Frank laughed and lay back on the long grass. "Lecture time, Joe. Bring a beer?" I shook my head, not taking my eyes off Weitchie.

"We were just discussing environmental ethics, Joe." Maude looked at me for a moment then turned back to the others. "It is true that many individuals through greed, fear, lust for comfort or power, and/or plain ignorance, are behaving in a way that is destructive of our culture and the resources of the planet. They sometimes behave like rodents gnawing on the roots, or like aphids sucking the juice of a plant, living selfishly for themselves without any regard for their neighbors or the welfare of the whole. Like cancer cells destroying their host. At the same time, there are others who are creatively building and evolving the same system or society. In reality there is always entropy and there is always growth in any living system. The question is, are some really destroying our eco-system, or is it just our own perception if we see it that way? Which do we emphasize in our perceptual filtering? Which side of the overall informational picture have we chosen to support with our actions?" She stopped to sip her hot chocolate, then continued. "We do have scientific data, but like the Bible and other religious or philosophical abstract material, one can argue both ways from that. Scientists are not infallible either. How to decide? And what response is appropriate if one accepts the perception of imminent destruction and builds a life style on that? Is violence then justified? Because we see others as violent does that make it correct behavior for us? And how do we define violence? Is hammering a spike into a tree that may injure someone violent or nonviolent? What of disabling equipment? How can we decide what is right?" She stopped, looking at them. I didn't understand much of what she said, then.

"And you are sure as fresh shit every morning going to tell us."

Maude took a deep breath. "We all filter what we choose to perceive in the world around us. Can you deny that?"

Frank sat up, slapping his old leather hat against one leg. "So what difference does it make? Does our differing choice of 'perceptional viewpoint' change anything? Does that stop the crazies and geek greed-heads from raping the whole earth? It does not. Philosophizing and preaching have always gone on side by side with the rape and destruction, most times supported it, lots of times the same people. Sure, a lot of people have their perceptions all screwed up. And their values. That's why they think it's all right to rip off the whole planet for their own pleasure." Frank tossed his cup to Jeb, shaking his head. "Beer's better. Look, listen to Joe here, he's been around watching the logging and the shit-fer-brains attempts to stop it. Ask him if good intentions, righteousness, or psychological insights will make any difference to those chainsaw rapists, bulldozer yahoos, or their greed-head bosses. Ask him! Ask him how they can be stopped."

They all turned to look at me in the gathering, violet-hued dusk. I turned away from watching her for a moment, noticing the flickering light of the little fire playing on Jeb's lean face. I sure didn't know what to say, but I tried, said what I was thinking. "I guess Weitchie doesn't much like fire. Figures. Standing over there by herself. I'm kind of surprised she lets you have even a little one like this. Sure must make her uncomfortable."

Maude laughed. "Just as I said, all a matter of perception. Of course Weitchie is not comfortable with fire, she perceives fire differently than we do. Fire has its place in nature, but not as a useful and comforting thing. That is a human perception. In nature fire may be necessary to kill competing vegetation, or insects, but it is primarily to be feared as uncontrollable. She lets us have a very small one to..."

"Shee-it! Perception, shitception. Action is the only thing can help us. Tell them, Joe, whether anyone has ever stopped a log sale, other than by buying up the whole thing at inflated prices or by making them pay double. Tell them whether anything has ever mattered but money."

Guess I was kind of getting into it, too, though I'd rather have just watched her. "It's true that they sure got a lot of money for the sections of forest that have been saved, and I hear folks down south are trying to raise a lot more money for more groves. Hope they get it in time. There's the parks, but I guess that land was mostly bought by the government. Those are the only way I've heard of for most of what's been saved. Guess you're right that money is pretty important."

"Right! If you're filthy rich from oil or some other exploitation of the earth or the dumb-ass workers, then you can save some trees. Either buy them direct or buy a politician. Salve a dirtied conscience by buying a dozen trees where the tourists will appreciate them. Yeah. Big deal. But that's right, it's the only way any redwoods have been saved. Those of us don't have money have got to try something different. Only chance we have is to make them pay, make them afraid it will cost more to take the trees than they will get out of them. Paranoia is a fine monkeywrench, best we poor folks have. Make them scared for their wallets. That's all they care about."

Didn't understand all of it, but Frank can be pretty persuasive. I was getting interested, but mostly I was still watching her, and it didn't look to me like Weitchie was happy with all the talk. She finally moved foreword, closer to the others, looking at Frank. "But what of my trees, friend Frank. Fire not hurt my trees, but humans do. This my mother place. Will they want take all these trees as they take all my others?"

"Hell no, they won't. We..." The whole group broke out in a lot of denials and were real serious, but after a bit they quieted and Weitchie raised one small hand again. "Not want spiking in my trees, not like your iron. But how they know my trees are here? Some human person has told those who would take trees? How can this be?" She looked around at the group, then turned to me. "Can you say, Joe?"

When she looked at me like that, and I thought about what I'd been saying to the other men, I could only stammer, "D-don't kn-now."

Maude stood. "How they found out about this grove does not matter now. It is private property and will be protected. That is final. We will..."

I couldn't breathe, let alone follow any more of the talk. I got to my feet. "Uh, I guess I'd better be going. Good to meet you, hope everything works out all right. If I can help.... Thanks for the chocolate. Night."

"Good night, Joe man."

"Night, Joe. Take it easy, eh?"

I stumbled through the ravine to my pickup, though I don't remember how. Just felt hollow and sick and wanted away from there. As far away as I could get, as quick as I could. When she looked at me like that and asked who had told...I should've minded my own damned business and kept my mouth shut.

Guess they hardly noticed me going because Michael told me later how they kept on with their talk. When the others had gone and the fire was out, he and Weitchie talked some more in his tent.

"Mik-ail, there is much I do not understand. Human people I know before, what you call Indians, and my prospector friend McEvoy, they not talk so like Maude and Frank. Much they say I do not understand. What is 'perception'?"

"Darling, don't worry about that; a lot of other people wouldn't understand them either. I don't always." He chuckled sleepily. "Mostly I was just looking at you and not paying much attention to their chatter."

"But I would know this."

"Okay, let me think. Perception is...oh hell. It's seeing or knowing, or well...how we see or know we know, that's better. Oh, I don't know either. Let's make love and go to sleep. Love you."

She sat up, looking out through the unzipped door. "McEvoy say most human are what he call 'Christian,' and so they hate me and my kind. Hate my trees and animal cousins and all things not like them. Why is this so?"

"Well, maybe because the clergy and priests are mostly all men and many are supposed to be celibate, so they don't like female things. They see nature and wild things as female. I don't know Weitchie and, anyway, not everybody is a celibate priest."

"What is 'celibate'?"

Michael laughed. "Honest, you don't want to know."

"So many humans now, I must know all of human ways. Then make forest right."

"Well, celibate means a man never lies with a woman, or even thinks about things like that."

She turned, staring at him. "Can not be so! You make joke with me?"

"No joke. Many men live like that, women too."

Weitchie shook her head. "But most human person see my trees as good and beautiful, is not so? Why they hate and want to destroy?"

"Some people see the profits that can be made as more good, more beautiful than anything else. Sounds kind of silly when I say it that way, but they see that many good things can be made of wood from trees, or bought with money from logging and milling trees."

"But what they make of wood from trees they see as more good than living tree? How can it be a thing dead is more good than live?"

"I tried to tell you before, they make benches, picnic tables, patios, decks, planter boxs, retaining walls, a lot of things. And houses."

"They need these things so much? Maybe they die, they not have such things? They have great trouble?"

"Well, no, don't think anybody would actually die."

"But trees die."

"I'm sorry, Weitchie darling, I can't explain. We'll save your trees. Nobody will make a patio or deck out of these. Come, lay down please."

As they settled down, the great horned owl called from the hillside. "Who-oo, whoo, whooo."

❦

Two days later, Monday, September 11th, was a work

day. I was still numb, couldn't remember Sunday at all. The boss took me and Buck off another job and sent us back there, to the stump dotted slope below the ravine, but it was well on into the morning by the time we arrived. The day was still and quiet with the sun a glowing spot in the gray sky. Maude, Michael and the others were just fixing lunch by the van when we arrived. They were not happy to see us. I was glad Weitchie couldn't leave her trees, or see me there.

As I took a hatchet and some stakes out of the dusty pickup, Buck went right over and checked out his tractor, then started it up. A few minutes behind us, the surveyor and his helper, along with a lawyer and a Sheriff's deputy, followed us in in their own vehicles. The other workers were getting their surveying equipment out of the vehicles as Maude, pulling a purple nylon jacket over her long white dress, came down the slope to where the surveyor was setting up his transit. The deputy and the lawyer got to her first. She stopped, staring at them.

"Just what is the meaning of this?"

The lawyer spoke first. "Dr. Kingsley? I'm Joshua Able, an attorney for Barron Mills. Here are my credentials." He held out some papers and Maude glanced at them. "I came out to inform you that your injunction has been lifted. I'm afraid you rather misinformed the judge and he changed his opinion when we gave him the correct information. The workers have been instructed to proceed and I advise you to leave immediately."

"How could you inform the judge that this was other than private land?"

"The ownership of this land has reverted to the state. I understand that your claim was based on an old homestead, but no one has worked this land or lived on it for over a century. Thus your claim is invalid. Do you suggest that you are a descendent or heir of the homesteader?"

"There is an heir of the original homesteader and I

represent her."

"And where is this person. What is her name, her legal address? Why doesn't she speak for herself?" He stood straighter, eye to eye with Maude. "I'm afraid that it appears as though you and your friends," he glanced at Jeb and Michael standing just behind Maude, "were being opportunistic in this matter. It appears that you found this valuable grove and discovered the old homestead deed and thought you could make a good thing of it. Naturally the judge could not countenance that. I wouldn't want to bring a civil suit against you in the matter. That would hardly be useful to anyone, would it?"

"Of all the distorted..."

"I must warn you, Doctor Kingsley, you do not have a case. You are in fact trespassing on public land and interfering with workers engaged in lawful enterprise to the detriment of their lawful employer. We would appreciate it if you folks would please find some other place to make your camp. There are many legitimate campgrounds in the area and along the coast. I must ask you to depart for your own welfare."

Maude started to reply but was drowned out by Buck throttling up his cat as it rolled forward toward them. When they didn't move out of the way, Buck stopped again, idling down. Maude spoke louder. "Lawyer Able, you are deliberately trying to intimidate me. I deeply resent that and I warn you we are not without resources to seek satisfaction. We have already begun a suit in the local court and it can be easily extended to cover your behavior. It may be there is some legal question of ownership here, but you have no right to begin work until that question is settled by the court. The owner is not a social person, but she has been living here off and on during the last century. In any case I do not believe you can set aside a homestead deed so easily."

"Doctor, the court has lifted your injunction, that is

all that needs saying. This deputy will maintain the peace and enforce the law."

"The deputy is here to uphold the law and the law gives us a reasonable amount of time to make our case. We have a right to be informed of the court's action and a reasonable time to react to it. Every word you say or moment longer you interfere with our activities is one more count I will add to the suit. You are warned."

The lawyer sighed and looked around. We just waited because they were standing right where the road was supposed to start. I guess the overweight deputy was getting tired of the whole thing, too, because when the lawyer turned to him, he finally spoke up.

"Ma'am, best you listen. This man has the right papers to begin work. I must ask you to step aside and move your vehicles so as not to interfere with them or endanger yourselves. Right now! Every minute you stand here arguing is costing this contractor money. He could sue for civil damages. Please take your people and leave. Now! I do not want to ask you again."

"Very well, I will not dispute with a sheriff's officer. I was going to contact our lawyer today in any case. We will go there now, and we will see who will be the loser in a civil suit." She turned and walked to the van, gesturing at the others to gather up their sleeping bags and other stuff.

It took them a little while to gather everything and jam it into the van. Michael seemed sort of stunned, but Maude spoke to him and he got in his fancy red sports car and followed the van back toward the highway. The lawyer and the deputy followed the others in their own cars.

The surveyor had already motioned his stickman on up the hill with his bundle of stakes and was leaning over his transit. Buck lowered the dozer blade and, revving the engine, began the new road toward the ravine and the two crumbling, gray outcrops of rock. I took my hatchet and a small sledge and went to help the stickman stake out the short route up into the ravine.

We stopped for lunch soon after, but I wasn't hungry. I thought there must be something I could do, but as we sat there, the overcast thickened overhead and so did my thoughts. Didn't know how I could get more numb. Just did.

❦

As Buck and I drove home that afternoon after starting the new road, I tried telling him that maybe we ought to save some of the ancient forest, especially groves like this one. He didn't want to hear it, frowned as he poured the last coffee from his big Thermos into the plastic cup. "Just logs, Joe-boy. Just more logs for cutting, hauling out and milling. That's the way it is. Always will be. Two by fours, two by sixes, just so many board feet of lumber."

"Don't agree, Buck. Might be good to save some. Lumber's useful, but they're cutting too fast. They can't grow new trees as fast as they're cutting the old ones. What are they going to do when all the big trees are gone?"

"Don't know, Joe; not our worry. Big shots will take care of it. They're planting a lot of trees all over, you know? Forest Service, state forest people, timber people, all planting more trees all over the place. Sure, might have to wait a few years on them before they're big enough for cutting, but they'll be along. Why save any of the old stuff when there's plenty of new coming on? We'll never run out of trees."

"Not the same, Buck. New trees they plant are all the same kind, acres and acres all the same. Just like growing corn back in the Midwest I saw one time. Acre after acre of the same, one kind of thing growing as far as a man could see. It's not right, not natural."

"Your getting to sound like them environmentalists, Joe. Mebbe you shouldn't read so much; it's not good for a working man."

"Scientists who study this sort of thing say if the old forests are destroyed they can never come back. Forests have grown over millions of years and once they're gone they can never come back, they say. Never know what new stuff they will find, medicines, things like that. They find new things all the time, and won't if it's all destroyed, all logged."

"Tell you plain, Joe: get a woman, settle down, and quit reading all that stuff. Watch TV. Won't hurt you. How 'bout that little redhead you mentioned the other day, back there in that redwood grove they're going to cut? She's maybe a little wild, living out in the woods, maybe a hippie sort, but you can tame her. Know you can. Listen to ol' Buck now, I ever steer you wrong?"

"I told you it's not like that."

"Why not? She selling those trees, she's loaded. Or more likely ol' Barron going to make the loot from those trees, but that's all right: rich woman would be too much trouble anyway. Go after her, Joe-boy. Be good for you."

"It's not me that matters, Buck: it's the trees. We should save some, especially redwoods. Takes centuries to grow a redwood grove. Two, three thousand years to replace a grove like that, and it wouldn't be really the same. Never be the same again."

He sighed and put the cup back on his Thermos. "Tell you again, Joe-boy: you talk like that, fellas ain't going to like it. Nor the boss. Not a bit. You can say what you want with me; I'm your buddy, but don't talk that way around the others. Boss hears about it...good by, Joe-boy."

"Maybe you're right, Buck. Guess there's nothing I can do anyway. Nobody would ever listen to a worker."

"You got it, Joe. Not our problem. Don't let a little chickee get you off into a lot of crazy ideas. Bachelor, shy like you, got to be a little careful there. Ol' Bowel Movement going to get it all anyway. No use fussing. Like they say on TV, beer and pretty women is what it's all about for us working stiffs." He started his song again. "What Barron wants, Barron gets..."

I pulled the pickup out onto the asphalt behind a couple of big freight trucks. "I could do without the singing, Buck."

Guess he was singing too loud to hear me.

❦

INTERLUDE: Barron holds the phone in one hand, elbow on his big steel desk, and runs the other hand through his thinning hair.

"Right, Josh. Keep that judge straightened out. Don't let him waffle on this one. I've got to have those trees....

"Right. I get those trees out of that grove and I can finish Owen's order he's been riding me about. Got to get that lumber to him or he'll raise all kinds of hell. He's a stockholder and I owe him money. Those big trees from that grove will give me a breather. You hear me. I've got to have those trees....

"Mabel's got the Timber Harvest Plan worked up; mostly copied the last one. I'll see it gets in today and I'll ask them for an Emergency Quick Review....

"Certainly. They always cooperate....

"Right. Take care of it. Bye, Josh."

Barron quickly dials another number. "This is Lelland Barron of Barron Mills. I would like to speak with Assemblyman Attos, if he is available....

"Yes, I'll hold....

"Wally, thanks for giving me a minute....

"Right. I'll make it brief. Got a small problem out here, a small misunderstanding. I believe you know Judge Smith?

"Is that right? Thought you knew him well, but didn't

know you played on the same high school football team. That's great! Great memories. Did you have a good season?...

"Yes, indeed. Oh yes, some people out here started a suit in Judge Smith's court to preserve some redwoods that were overlooked some years ago. A small grove in an isolated canyon. They don't really have any grounds, but they have some money and a big city lawyer, you know how it goes....

"Right, happens more and more often these days. Anyway, I thought a word from you would help to clarify the matter and...

"Exactly. I know you understand how important it is to keep the mill running full time, with all the jobs and families depending on the mill, and the local economy in your district...

"Right. The Timber Harvest Plan is in, and I'm sure they'll act on it quickly. They are always very helpful....

"Right. Thank you very much, sir. I always know I can count on you....

"Right. I won't forget. Have I ever?...

"Just right. Bye, Wally." Barron chews his lip for a moment then turns to the computer, striking the keys and calling up a file, then another.

❦

6

THREAT

...Should never have told Buck or any of the other men about Weitchie's grove. They're awful gossips, and they sure didn't understand. Or want to. I didn't really understand at first either, and later, when I began to get caught up in all that was happening, it was too late. As soon as Mr. Barron knew about those trees.... Never cared about anything this way before, didn't know how to act, just felt helpless.

All ancient, native forest is precious and somehow, deep inside, I always knew that. And there have always been a few other people around who felt that way, too. Besides the government making some parks and people with money buying up groves here and there, mostly small ones, there's a history of protest, especially over the last twenty years or so. Never did understand that before, but I do now. Some of the protesters have been pretty ingenious in the things they think of doing, actually sitting in front of bulldozers, or chaining themselves to trees, and demonstrating at mills, docks, and government offices. Real clever most times, but sometimes they get sent to jail.

Maude tried getting a good lawyer and going to court to settle ownership of Weitchie's land, but courts are slower than a banana slug. Come to think of it, the slugs don't stop for coffee breaks and two hour lunches. While Maude was going to court, Frank was recruiting, and he's pretty good at that. Some of his new friends didn't wait: they showed up the next morning before Buck and I drove in to work on the short piece of new road to the ravine.

It was Tuesday, September 12th, and the clouds were lower than the day before. Mist was blowing and, as we drove in, dawn crept silently over the land shining and soft as pearl-gray velvet. Didn't see any of the ones I knew except for Frank. Must have been a dozen of them, mostly young, in jeans, denim jackets, and t-shirts, grouped in front of Buck's big yellow cat parked on the slope by the entrance to the ravine. Buck wasn't happy about seeing them....

"God damn, Joe, would you look at that. Lousy damned hippies and jerks all over the place. Those assholes better not have messed with my Gertrude." Buck jumped out, leaving the truck door open, and ran up the slope toward his tractor before I had the pickup stopped. After parking next to the other cars and taking the key out of the ignition, I closed the doors and followed, slower, looking at the small, hand lettered signs some of the protesters held and waved about.

NO COMPROMISE!
REVERENCE FOR DIVERSITY!
HAYDUKE LIVES!

I didn't know what that last one meant.

There were just the two of us, Buck and me. We didn't figure more men were needed for cutting road because naturally the cat does most of the work. I just come along in case Buck needs something or there's a little chopping or digging that needs doing. Safer with two men, but it didn't look so safe today with all those people gathered in a clump in front of that big dozer blade. Took some courage standing there. Buck wouldn't actually run someone over, but he might think about it. Might even want to, and I could see he was pretty hot when I caught up with him as he crawled out from underneath the machine.

"Everything okay, Buck?" It was hard talking over the chanting as Buck stood up, dusting off his Levi jeans and glaring at the protesters.

"Yeah. Doesn't look like the bastards hit my Melanie, but I'll have it all checked out in a minute. Then we'll see about these noisy bastards."

Michael and Frank walked down from the ravine, looking at me. "Good morning, Joe." Michael gave me half a grin, seemed sort of embarrassed as he yelled over the noise. "Doesn't look like there'll be any road building today. These people showed up about an hour ago. Made such a racket, they woke me up. Guess they're friends of Frank's." Frank just grinned at me.

"Where're your other friends?"

"Maude and Jeb are in town. Maude sent Clare and Hensley on home on the bus."

The people had quieted, wanting to hear what we said, and Frank, who really likes to grandstand, was grinning from ear to ear and talking even louder than usual in that hoarse voice of his. "No more road, Joe. Go back and tell your bosses they're finished on this job. They're not going to get these trees. Take your big yellow toy and go on home. This is not..."

Buck started the cat just then, revving it while he stared at Frank, then back to his dials. Makes a lot of noise if you're standing right alongside and the people started chanting again at the same time. I didn't know what to do. First time I ever got in the middle of one of these things.

Buck lowered the blade into the ground and started the ponderous machine moving forward. A few of the protesters moved out of the way and then I could see that one bunch of four was sitting on the ground with bicycle cable and heavy chains wrapped around them, all padlocked together. I hadn't see them behind the blade at first with the others in the way. "Buck!" He didn't hear me, or didn't want to, so I jumped onto the track and into the seat beside him, yelling in his ear. "That bunch is all chained together. They can't move!"

He grinned even wider and yelled back, "I see 'em. Just like a bunch of bananas. Never thought I'd be a banana plucker." He laughed. I jumped back down to the ground and ran ahead though I don't know what I could have done.

Buck was cutting a wide switchback across the slope approaching the bottom of the ravine and he still had a little ways to go, filling in the brook and building up a ramp to get through between those two crumbling rock outcrops. He kept on pushing piles of dirt and rock closer and closer to the group chained together. Guess he thought they would panic. They didn't.

The whole thing went on for an hour and twenty-five minutes. The protesters singing and threatening to throw clods and rocks, and Buck, grinning like crazy, pushing the dirt closer until some of it fell on the feet of the two young fellows nearest the tractor. It wasn't really as dangerous as it looked because Buck is really good; he's had a lot of experience and knows within an inch where that blade is, but I don't know if the people chained together knew that. Anyway they couldn't move if they wanted to. Guess that's what commitment means, getting yourself into a thing like that.

Buck kept on piling dirt around them as Frank and the others sang crazy songs, yelled, or cursed him. I just stood to one side with Michael, watching. We were both pretty nervous. In fact, I was shivering. Wasn't worried about Buck, but all the noise and shouting in that open space got to me real bad. Seemed the whole world had suddenly become angry. More than angry: about to explode. I'd never felt like that before. Been close to a couple of brawls, but this didn't feel like that. Near wiped me out.

Michael wasn't much better. He kept turning to me and yelling for me to stop it. I just shook my head. Frank glanced at me once in a while, still grinning like crazy. In between talking with his people, he was yelling crazy things at Buck: "If you had a bigger prick and knew how to use it, you wouldn't need that dozer.... Can't make it with women?.... This your kinder, gentler America?.... Bet you couldn't cut a marshmallow if you was off your machine." Yelling a lot of crazy stuff like that. Don't remember half of it.

Buck finally had the chained-together protesters almost surrounded with piled up dirt and rock. He stopped with the blade one yard in front of the four of them, stared for a minute, then shut the tractor off and climbed down, looking at me. It was suddenly very quiet. "Hey, Joe, how come you're just standing there. Go get a bolt cutter. We got to get these stumps here unchained so's I can get them outa the way. Go on. Head on in and get me the cutters. What you waiting on? Maybe bring a torch too, just in case."

Buck was sort of my boss, and I'm supposed to help him, fetch things and like that, but right then I was too numb to think or do much of anything. He walked up with a heavy wrench in one hand and gave me a friendly shove. "Go for it, Joe-boy. Come on, we got us an audience for once, gotta keep the show rolling. Go get the bolt cutters, and maybe that deputy might enjoy the show too, you reckon? Go on in and find out, okay?"

"Uh, yeah Buck. I'll be right back." That's what I always said when he sent me after something. Those people all watched as I went to the pickup.

The Sheriff's Office has bolt cutters and torches for times like this, so after calling them I just called in to the office and then drove back. It was getting close to lunch time when I got there, and the protesters were sitting talking among themselves in front of the cat. Buck was sitting quietly off to one side watching them, the wrench on the ground beside him. Guess they'd all run out of things to say to each other.

I didn't see Frank around as the two Sheriff's cars drove up right behind me, parking beside the protester's cars. A Highway Patrol cruiser came in right behind them. Their dust rose, brown against the gray clouds.

Buck walked down to meet us as the six deputies and two Highway Patrol officers got out of their cars. The protesters watched, waving signs and chanting softly. A tall, skinny fellow I guess was their leader and two women, one of them with auburn red hair loose over a green blouse, walked down toward the officers. I'd hardly noticed them before.

One deputy stayed by the car with the radio mike in his hand watching as the others spread out and started up the slope. The big deputy in front of the group had a bullhorn, but everything was still pretty quiet for a minute, I remember hearing a crow grawking down the draw to the east. The deputy raised the horn to his thick lips. "You people are illegally interfering with workmen engaged in lawful activity. I want all of you to line up over here with your identification. When I have seen that ID, I want you all to leave peaceably." The bullhorn echoed off the other slope across the draw as if there were two men yelling, one voice a little deeper than the other.

One of the women walking down the slope called out, "Nothing wrong with our hearing officer. You can shut your horn off."

The deputy did. "Very well, line up over here." They didn't.

The other young woman, the redhead, spoke up as the three of them faced down the deputy. "You have been misinformed, Officer Welch, these workmen are engaged in an illegal activity. This is private land. Tell them to..."

The burly deputy interrupted her. "I know about the situation here, Miss Annerman. I called the court before we came out. The ownership of this property is in question, but meanwhile these workmen are within their rights. Now line up quickly and we won't arrest all of you this time."

The tall protester laughed. "Come on, Sergeant Welch, you know better than that. These workers are just trying to get to that stand of trees in there before the owner can get her claim straightened out through your slug-slow court. She'll win in the end and you know it."

"I'll not say it again, Mister Moses, line up with your IDs or I'll arrest you all for obstructing lawful enterprise. Now!" He handed the bullhorn to another deputy and pulled out his note pad. "I want to see ID on all of you."

The three looked at each other then around the slope. The officers stood in a semicircle facing them. The tall, slender fellow shrugged. "If you insist, Welch, we've all got our ID with us. You won't find anybody interesting here, but while you're busy writing us all up in your little note pad, how about explaining a few things. Like why does the Sheriff's Office always side with the loggers, even when we win most of the court cases and appeals in the end?"

The sergeant ignored him and started writing down the names of the protesters, beginning with the tall fellow and the two women who kept asking him all kinds of questions as they held out their driver's licenses.

When the protesters that could move were written up and standing a little to one side, the sergeant walked over to the group chained together before the dozer blade. "Okay. You want to unlock?" No one moved. "Start cutting." He motioned to the deputies who carried bolt cutters.

It took a while, but when they had all six loose, the deputies slapped cuffs on them and started them toward the cars. The rest of the protesters set up a howl and the sergeant reached for the bullhorn again. "All clear out of here or face arrest for obstructing an officer. Right now!"

I guess there wasn't much of anything anybody could usefully do then. The ones that were loose backed away from the patrol cars, and as soon as the six cuffed protesters were loaded, the others started leaving.

Soon as everybody was gone, with the dust settling, Buck and I sat down by the pickup to eat our lunch. He was watching a buzzard circling high overhead, watching us. He didn't have much to say this time, just sat there grinning.

❦

With Fall coming on, the days were getting shorter. Dark came quick in the narrow canyon sheltering Weitchie's grove. Went by that evening after work and found all the others gathered in the clearing, sitting in a rough circle, including the tall fellow and the two women who were leaders of the protest. Weitchie stood by her tree holding hands with Michael. She smiled at me but didn't say anything. Maude was bringing everyone up to date.

"The injunction is in place again. The judge was misinformed by the timber interest's lawyer, which I gather is not unusual, but you would know more about that than I." The tall fellow nodded. "I understand that your friends were not booked, only held for awhile and then released at the end of the working day?" He nodded again. "Now we must decide on our further course of action. Jeb and I will return to town in the morning and do what we can, but first I want to know where you three stand on 'monkey wrenching,' sabotaging loggers' equipment, spiking trees, that type of illicit activity." She glanced at Frank. "I tell you plainly, we want nothing to do with that."

The three protesters looked at each other, then the redheaded woman spoke for them. "You must understand there are different groups in the area, and, while we try to cooperate with each other, we have philosophical differences. Some of us approve of civil disobedience as long as it is nonviolent, others follow a different path. We three actually come from different groups, so I can't make any promises for anyone else. For myself, I say anything that works. My friends sometimes disagree."

"I see. I was afraid of that. If you were recruited by Frank, then it is obvious that none of you have any great respect for working within the law. Anarchy is indeed abroad in the land, and growing."

The tall fellow spoke up. "Excuse me, but that is not entirely correct, Dr. Kingsley. Actually, most of us agree with you and try to work within the system, using appeals, injunctions and lawsuits. But sometimes, frankly, as in this case, we need help from the others to stall road building and logging until the courts can act or appeals be heard. The system of law is sometimes too slow. We condemn no one."

Maude looked at Frank. "I suppose that is the way of things in these times. Our small group is also divided."

Frank, sitting on the ground by the big tree with his arms around his knees grinned up at her. His hat lay on the ground behind him. "You can bet your precious long butt we're divided. If I hadn't called on my friends and acted today, they'd been into the ravine and ready to start cutting these trees in the morning. We slowed them, but you better move that lawyer of yours, tell him to get his fancy shyster ass in gear real quick. Those rapists will sure as regular morning shit be back. There's no end to their greed."

"Frank, our lawyer is aware of the need for haste.

Please control your natural tendencies a little longer and the situation will be settled to everyone's satisfaction. Will you do that?"

"Long as it stays quiet around here, but if that shit-eating bastard of a dozer operator comes and cranks up that monster rape machine again, we'll do whatever we need to do to keep him from this canyon. That's..."

"Frank, please stop using such inflammatory and scurrilous language and listen to me. What was done this morning was dangerous." Jeb and Michael and one of the women agreed. "Those people could have been subjected to violence. They..."

"Dammit!" Frank jumped up, both arms raised. "Can't you see that we've already been subjected to violence? All our lives we've been betrayed, over and over. Along with the forests, the wild places, the whole planet, our sanctity has been dirtied and our naturalness distorted. We're all of us fucking insane, living in this insane system of greed and destruction! Our values have been skewed by these hypocritical, mother-hating, earth-raping big companies. By their advertisers, the TV, the politicians they own, all those other bullshit artists that twist everything, calling black white and white black. How can anyone know what's right anymore? Can't you see that? Gods above help us!" He shook his head. "There's no hope. None at all, if people like you won't wake up and open your eyes and see what's going on. Gods!" Frank turned away, leaning both hands against the mother tree, his face against the soft reddish bark. Then he straightened and turned back. He was crying.

"They want to cut this. This beautiful living tree. Destroy forever this whole grove. And for what? Greed! Profit! Obscene, filthy profit!" He turned back to the tree, leaning his forehead against it, shoulders shaking.

No one said anything for a while and it was quiet except for a small flock of birds, chattering and gorging themselves in a clump of salmonberry. I wondered what the birds were discussing. Back by the ferns, I had been mostly watching Weitchie as she sat with Michael on that half buried buttress root beside her mother tree. Guess the newcomers had been introduced to her before I got there, and I couldn't tell whether they believed her or not, but they seemed real impressed, looking around at the grove and watching her real close.

Weitchie finally stood, breaking the silence, looking at Maude. "I tell you so, Maude, all of you: Frank loves my trees. Joe there does, too." They turned, looking at me, mostly frowning as they recognized me. "Come sit by me, Joe. I tell you all, do not have anger for Frank and Joe. Both have a part in what is to be. They love me and my trees. You will see." They extended their circle to include me as I walked over and sat on the ground close to the tree. And close to her.

"I am not knowing all you speak of, appeals, courts, such things I do not know, but I think is good doing what must be done. All my forest of great trees they have taken. Now they want these few are left for me. This is very sad, very bad thing for all life. Why they kill my trees? For what they need do that? Some human say trees are sacred, but I say no one thing sacred because all things are so. Why human not understand that? Why want kill so much? Not good for you all Mother Earth life be so changed."

Michael reached and took her hand. "Darling, don't worry. We'll get it all straightened out soon. They won't come any farther, and when it's over we can fix the damage they've done. Just be patient."

"Yes, Mik-ail, patient I know, that I know well. But this my only place in your reality. This tree is gone, I am gone. No more. For a time I exist in Dream but fade away without body in living tree. So long as my mother tree is well she gives me nurture and I can live in other, Dream Reality, but if she is gone, I am gone. You hear what I say?"

Michael nodded, looking real troubled. The others agreed they understood.

She looked at each of us, then off into the distance. "In other reality of my kind, is all things very good, much of joy and beauty. Some have differences, as you say, some anger is there, but no one does death to any other thing. We do not need killing of tree for making shelter, nor death of animal for food. All is different and good there, but our bodies must live here. We are of the Earth and must keep our roots in healthy Earth. Without, we can not long exist in Dream. All I meet there must have body in safe, nurturing place: some in lakes, streams, or big salty water. Others leave bodies in the earth or rock. Some have other ways. You understand?" She looked around at us again. I sure didn't, but I wanted to. Never wanted anything more.

"Before you have fire and iron tools and begin cutting trees, all was good for us. But now in Dream Time, in last turnings before Maude wake me, very few there in that place, our last refuge. Before, when I am very little dryad and first go to that reality there were many. Now very few. You human, you disturb all of Mother Earth. Very few places you not disturb with machines and too many people. Very few places left." A tear fell from her chin, and another, and another. Perhaps others could not see them falling in the fading light, but, sitting so close, I could. I never knew a man could feel so helpless. So completely helpless.

Had trouble sleeping that night, when I got home, tossed and turned, never really got any rest at all.

❦

The boss sent Buck and me back again the next day, Wednesday. Told us to go right on. I didn't know what to say, tongue-tied as usual with him, but I knew it was wrong. He glared at me as he told us in front of the other workers, then grinned like a shark. The other men didn't look at me at all. Guess I'd said too much about trees, but what else could I do?

When we got there no one was around. There weren't even any cars, and we guessed they were all in town. As I climbed out of the truck and started toward the tractor, I thought of Weitchie all alone with us getting ready to cut the drag path through the ravine into her canyon. I was sick.

"God damn, fucking..." As I walked up to his cat, Buck was cursing in an undertone as he checked it over. Somebody had fixed it real good, and that big powerful piece of machinery wasn't going anywhere for a long while. They had bashed, cut, or torn loose everything they could. I had to sit down on the ground to keep from falling. It looked like Frank and his friends had been busy, though I found out later Frank himself didn't have anything to do with it. Never did learn who did, but I thanked them.

After Buck had checked over what he could, I drove him back to town. He was in a foul mood when we started, didn't say anything for a while, just sat stiffly and drank his coffee. Gulping it. He softened as we turned south on the smooth black asphalt, heading for town and the shop yard.

"Reckon a man's got to be philosophical sometimes, Joe, but it bothers me real bad when they pick on a dumb machine. Guess I can sort a understand how they feel though, pretty tough trying to take on ol' BM and the whole system. Guess they get desperate sometimes. That right, Joe-boy? You went by and talked with them again last night?"

"Yes, Buck, I talked with them. Mostly just listened. Some of them are real frustrated and angry."

"Figures they'd be frustrated trying to beat the system. Dumb bet. Ought to relax and enjoy it. Who ever had it better? Eh, Joe? You read history. Who ever had it better than us?"

"Maybe because some things are good, most people eating regular and all, some want everything even better. Want everything right, but not everything is. There are still things not right in this country, Buck."

"Ah hell, Joe, what you want for Chris' sake? Only ones don't have food and homes are the goof-offs, maybe a few crazies, people not willing to work a little. Anybody who's willing to play along and do some work, everything is fine. None of those assholes yesterday looked hungry or nothing. Probably most of them rich kids, got college degrees and everything."

"It's not just food, Buck."

"What else then? Ass? There's all the nooky anybody'd want just for the taking. Some like you get yourselves all frustrated, but it's your own damn doings. Why take it out on a dumb machine and a couple of working stiffs like us?

"There's other things."

"Like what? For God's sake, what do you want? C'mon, Joe, you're just another hardhat redneck like me. Why'd you want to get a thing going for these redwood trees? They're just two-by-fours for making benches, decks, and fence posts. Sure, we got to save a few for the tourists, along the roads and around the parks; but the rest're waiting for cutting. That's what they're there for, why get yourself all worked up? There's plenty left in the park." He gave a disgusted snort. "Let's get a beer after work at Sardi's. You know that tall waitress's got her eye on you. Why not give her a tumble, Joe? Do her a favor. She's no beauty queen, but what the hell, they all got what a man needs. I'll buy the first round o' Coors."

"No thanks, Buck, don't feel so good. Not used to all this hassle, I guess. Want to get on home soon as work's over. Rest and think on things."

"Joe-boy, thinking is what you don't need. Doing to much of that already. C'mon, I'll buy. Don't offer like that every day."

"Thanks, Buck, but I really want to get home."

"Okay. I give up. Your loss." He put the cap back on his big Thermos.

A few drops of rain fell, spotting the thick dust on the windshield as we drove through town and pulled into the shop yard in the middle of the morning.

❦

INTERLUDE: Barron is furious. He grips the phone with white hands. His face is splotched as he stands behind his big steel desk.

"Dammit, Josh, you've got to do something. There's got to be a way to get to that damned judge. Find it! I've got to have those logs....

"No. You know damned well I can't wait. I have to have those logs. Now!...

"And where are those heirs? You think there might...must be somebody around named McEvoy." He sits in the padded swivel chair and leans back, raising one arm over his head.

"Right. Do it. Check the Greater San Francisco phone book, LA, Orange County, San Diego. Check everywhere. Find some people named McEvoy and promise them whatever you have to, but just do it. We can always work things out later if anybody has a problem....

"That's right, Josh, go for it. Find somebody. I'm counting on you....

"Right. Let me know as soon as you have anything at all, and I'll send the crew in to start cutting those big trees. Not a lot of trees in that grove, but they're big, a lot of board feet there Josh, a whole lot....

"Good, Josh, and thanks a lot. I'll not forget. Bye."

Barron rises. Pushing the chair back, he walks over to the big picture window where he stands with one hand against the wall, looking out and rubbing his forehead under his thinning hair.

Three crows fly across the narrow valley and the bisecting highway, through the dozen thin columns of smoke and steam rising slowly from the mill and the small town. Just above the height of the surrounding rounded hills, the smoke flattens, disappearing into the colorless, overcast sky.

7

REASSURANCE

...Weitchie's grove was so well hidden in a canyon whose entrance was through a narrow ravine, it never would have been found if I hadn't got curious and talked about it. It's my fault Mr. Barron found out, and I have to live with that. Never in my life felt so helpless; couldn't think of anything useful I could do. Couldn't see how one man could do anything anyway.

Maude told me the grove was hidden by some higher power, something like that. She believed that only those who were somehow supposed to could ever have found Weitchie or her grove. I couldn't believe that. If it was true, and there was something guiding everything that happened, why let me find the grove and lead the loggers right to it? Seemed like a dumb idea. Might as well put up a big sign. I didn't understand things very well then, I still don't, but it doesn't matter now. Now I know what I'm supposed to do, and I know that things can change, sometimes much faster than anyone can guess.

Buck and I saw a few cars, but everything was quiet and none of the people were around as I helped Buck get the damaged tractor loaded on the low-boy trailer and headed back into the shop. Had to use a winch to pull it on and off. The boss was real angry, must've cost him plenty. Cloud cover was burning off next afternoon as Buck and I carried another cat in. I was beginning to feel somewhat better, sleeping better, too. It was Friday and we left the tractor to the watchman for the weekend....

Monday, the sun rose in a clear sky. The boss sent us in to finish filling the narrow mouth of the ravine so we could get the big cat in to skid the logs out. I didn't want to, but what could I say? When Buck and I turned off the paved highway, we found an old beat up junker of a car blocking the old logging road, all locked up and nobody around. Took us a while, prying a wing open and getting the brake off so we could roll it to the side of the road. When we finally got to the job at 8:15, they were waiting for us.

I think there were fifteen or sixteen this time, but with all the noise they made, it seemed like more. Didn't see anyone I knew at first. Don't know where the others all came from. Found out later Michael was with Weitchie and Frank was acting as lookout, staying out of sight.

Some of the protesters had chained themselves together again, right in the narrow mouth of the ravine, sitting in a clump just past the pile of dirt Buck had pushed up before, and this time some were chained to the tractor itself. Seemed crazy to me. They were chanting slogans as we got out of the dusty green pickup. The logging crew came in right behind us in their own trucks ready to start cutting the trees in the canyon.

The protesters were waving signs again, one big one in red letters that looked real professional read:

IT'S THE ONLY WORLD WE HAVE
LOVE IT OR GET THE HELL OFF!

Where would anybody go?

Other smaller, rougher, hand lettered signs read:

NO MORE COMPROMISE!
1,000 HAYDUKES!

REVERENCE FOR DIVERSITY!
ED'S BIRTHDAY A HOLIDAY!
JESUS WAS A HIPPIE TOO!

Buck was really hot as he jumped out of the truck and ran to check the new tractor. The loggers looked angry, too, climbing out of their trucks. We all stayed close as we walked up by the tractor. Buck climbed onto the seat, and one of the protesters started playing a guitar and the rest started singing. Reminded me a lot of a revival meeting I went to a long time ago. Preacher wanted young people to go to South America and help the Indians, preach at them or something like that.

Luckily Buck didn't find anything wrong with his new machine, but he didn't dare start it up with them chained like that to the blade. Really crazy. Made him even angrier and he stood up on the track, trying to yell over the singing of the protesters.

"You punks want to get your asses kicked? You've come to the right place. Unlock and get the hell out of here or else." Singing as loud as they were, I don't think anybody could hear him but me and the loggers. After a minute of glaring at them, Buck turned to me and yelled, "Get those bolt cutters, Joe, you got work to do." This time we had brought our own bolt cutters, but I shook my head, not knowing what to say.

He looked disgusted for a moment, then jumped down and headed for the pickup. I followed with one of the loggers. When Buck got to the truck and pulled out the big cutters, the logger caught his arm. "Ought to get the deputies, Buck. Let them handle this. Get in trouble, we do it ourselves."

"Get the fucking deputies if you want, I got work to do." Buck started back up the slope toward the protesters. The logger went with him, but I hesitated a minute before following. I was feeling sick and hollow again. The noise got even louder as we approached. Don't know how it could, but it did.

As Buck and the loggers paused before the clump of protesters, Michael came running from one side, breathing hard and grabbing my arm. "You've go to stop them, Joe. These people are really crazy. Frank's been talking to them, and that red-headed Annerman woman, getting them all worked up. They're angry and somebody might get hurt. C'mon, you've got to do something. I'll help."

I wasn't thinking good with all the noise and my mind was blank as a wad of cotton, but he pulled on my arm and I went with Michael toward the protesters chained in front of the steel blade. Buck was already trying to cut one link of chain and the loggers were standing close together in a half circle behind him, glaring at the protesters under their hardhats, their fists clenched. The link of chain Buck was working on was hanging right between the breasts of a husky young woman, and maybe Buck was a little free with his hands as he tried to get the cutter set in a loop of the chain. I could see between two loggers as she pushed his hand away with one of hers and slapped his face with the other. He reached out and slapped her, not real hard, but the young man next to her grabbed the bolt cutter, pulling it out of Buck's hand, and passed it back to others. Buck slapped him hard and leaned over, reaching for the cutter. Michael, meanwhile, had let go of me and was pushing through the loggers. Maybe he couldn't see what was happening, but he jostled Buck and the two of them fell onto the chained protesters. After that everything got mixed up. People were pushing, shoving, and yelling. I tried to get to Michael and Buck, but some protester with a sign in his hand turned towards me and, as I dodged him, I lost my balance and fell against a logger standing against the side of the tractor and swinging at anybody who came near. The last thing I saw was a big fist with a gold wedding band on the third finger as it smashed into my face.

When I came to there was a small army of uniforms

all around me. Sheriff's deputies, Highway Patrolmen and others were breaking up scuffles and handcuffing people. The noise was still fierce; the protesters were singing again, but the action slowed as they went limp, not trying to resist. One young fellow near me got carried away and swung at an officer. He was face down on the dirt an instant later, cuffed.

By the time I picked up my hardhat and got off the ground, rubbing my chin, the officers already had a van full of protesters and were dragging others down to the cars. They were real efficient. Found out later they had been trained for it, practiced on each other. Of course the protesters weren't fighting anymore, just going limp and singing. I couldn't see Michael or any of the others I'd met.

The officers had also handcuffed one of the loggers. I think it was the one who'd hit me; maybe he'd swung on a cop, too. Buck got that straightened out. It all took a while, but soon there was nothing left but settling dust, torn up signs, and the eight of us standing, some still breathing hard.

Buck looked at me for a long moment. "You all right, Joe?" I nodded. "Looks like you're gonna have a right fine lump on your chin. Let's get back to work, day's more than half gone and we got to move us some dirt today. Boss'll be pissed sure, mostly cause he missed the fun." Buck laughed and rubbed a bleeding scratch on his cheek. "Some o' them little women was sure hot. Feels like one of them got me. Ah well, had my fun. Come on, back to work."

"Maybe eat some lunch first, Buck? It's near noon."

He looked at me and grinned. "You eat, Joe-boy, I'm working." He started up the tractor and I went to straighten out and replace the survey stakes for him. One of the cutest tricks I've heard of is changing the stakes after a surveyor has laid out a road. Heard of one place where the dozer operator went over a low cliff following stakes that had been moved. It was no problem here though, because the skid road had to go into the narrow space between the two rock outcrops anyway and I knew where all the stakes were supposed to be.

The loggers stopped for lunch first, then got their long bar chainsaws and other equipment out of their truck and started up the ravine.

I found out later from Michael that he had been hurt, too, and had staggered into the grove, where he lay down with blood running from a cut on his temple. Guess he was a mess when Weitchie found him by the first of her trees. She took off the purple flannel shirt, dipping it into the cold water of the brook and wiping his face to stop the bleeding. Hate to think what might have happened if the loggers had gone in right away and found her naked.

"Weitchie?"

"Yes, Mik-ail. Best you come more in among my trees. Some those people might come. I help you."

She was real small but strong, and, leaning on her, he got up and staggered deeper into the grove, gaining strength as he went. The bleeding got worse, a messy kind of wound. Weitchie led him to the pool and, wringing out the shirt, held it to his head.

"Darling, hold the cloth to the back of my neck. Might help more. My gods, that shirt's a mess. Go get your other clothes; I can hold this. Some of those other men were loggers and they might come in to look around. Please." She nodded and left him for a few minutes, returning in the purple pants and blouse Maude had bought for her.

"Darling, don't worry, they got ahead of us for a little, but Maude and the lawyer will get it all straightened out. We have justice in this land. They won't get away with what they're trying to do. Okay? You're brave."

She nodded and had just sat down beside him, holding his hand, when three chain saws started up all at once, their coughing, whining roar bouncing off the walls of the canyon. Limbs started crashing to the ground.

"Weitchie, don't..." She screamed. He held her there the rest of the afternoon until the loggers quit for the day. Guess it was like one of us having our fingers or toes cut off.

❦

The way it worked out, with the loggers getting a late start, they'd only dropped one of the big trees, trimming and bucking it to length. The next morning was sunny and bright, and they had cut another tree down and had started topping a third. I was standing at the entrance to the ravine watching Buck rattling back in after dragging the first huge section of log out to the road. Maude, Jeb, and Frank arrived with their new lawyer. He was a tall fellow in a business suit with polished shoes. Looked odd out there.

The lawyer waved for the others to wait at the entrance to the ravine as he went on up to the loggers and yelled over the whine of the chainsaws, motioning for them to shut off the motors. I guess they figured he had a right, being in a snappy suit and all, or maybe they were just curious. Anyway, they shut off the saws and set them down. Guess the topper high up in the tree saw the others and shut off his saw. He hung there in his harness, watching.

"I am an attorney for the owner of this land and I have a new injunction barring any further work here. Right here." He held the papers out to them. "You men shut it down. Get your equipment together and get out of here."

"Now just a minute, mister, whoever you are, we're doing the work we're supposed to be doing and we had enough hassle here yesterday. Don't want anymore today. Why don't you just move out of our way? Head on back before you get your fancy suit messed up." All five of them on the ground glared at the attorney. He held his ID out, staring right back.

Thought there might be more violence, but I walked on up the ravine anyway. Buck had throttled down his tractor and was watching closely and when I looked back at him, Maude, Jeb, and Frank were right behind me.

As we came up behind him, the loggers had set their equipment down and were threatening the attorney, one drawing his fist back. Just as it looked like trouble, their boss walked around the tractor. He whistled real loud to get everybody's attention, then just waved his hand across his face. They backed off and started gathering up their equipment, mumbling among themselves as the top man slid down from his high perch. If that lawyer was a little nervous, he didn't show it. Really cool.

After the loggers and their boss left, the lawyer and the others walked into the narrow valley, ducking under the big tree that had been dropped against the side of the canyon. Redwoods have to be dropped carefully or they just split and break up.

Buck backed the tractor down toward the road and I was standing by him as he shut it down. "You drive on in, Buck, I'll get home somehow. Uh, see you tomorrow morning. Tell the boss I'm taking the rest of the day off."

He gave me a big grin. "She still in there, Joe? Sure, go on. I'll make it okay with the boss. You go and see your sweetie. She might be kind of upset with all this stuff going on, right? You go comfort her, fella, and don't let that city man get in the way. What's he got that you don't have more of, eh? And if I don't see you in the morning I'll sure know why." He laughed and started toward the pickup, then turned back. "Got the keys?"

"Oh sure, here. Thanks, Buck, see you." I tossed him the keys and hurried after the others into the canyon.

Weitchie was pale. She looked kind of splotched with

her red coloring and parts of her face and arms white. Hurt me to see her like that, but I guess it figured what with the cutting that had been done. The birds and butterflies seemed quiet, and I didn't see any animals at all, but she was still watching for me when I pushed through the ferns. She smiled and waved.

"Hi Joe. Come sit with us."

The others looked grim and sad at the same time, especially Frank. Don't know how I could tell what he was feeling with all that hair hiding his face, but it was plain he wasn't happy. Guess they all felt for Weitchie, too. Michael had gotten a big gauze pad taped onto his temple but didn't look bad otherwise. He was sitting with one arm around Weitchie's waist. Jeb was fixing some coffee as they reluctantly made a place for me.

The lawyer was tall and lanky and had an expressionless sort of deadpan face, but his eyes looked spooked as he stood there staring at Weitchie as if she might blow up or something. Bad as I was feeling, I had to stifle an urge to laugh and choked instead. Maybe it was just being able to relax as I sat on the ground, or perhaps the smell of Jeb's coffee mingling with the smells of the grove set me off. Guess Jeb knew what I was thinking because he set the coffee pot down and slapped me on the back, grinning. Weitchie was smiling a little, too, and looking at me, when I got my breath back and looked up. That took my breath away again. Being around her.... Wanted to help but couldn't think of anything I could say or do.

Maude took the first cup from Jeb. "I'm glad we got here when we did, at least. I am very sorry it took so long, Weitchie, and that we could not manage to get here sooner. It must have been very difficult for you."

"I live okay for this moment, Maude. Will they come again?"

"Hell no! Those bastards try again, they...oh shit!" Frank turned away, leaning against the mother tree.

Maude shook her head, braids swinging across her breasts. "No. This time I am sure we have stopped them. We will know for certain tomorrow. Attorney Jones," she nodded toward the well-dressed fellow, "will see the judge again first thing in the morning. I do not fully comprehend all this legal maneuvering myself, but that is correct, is it not, Mr. Jones?"

The lawyer slowly pulled his eyes off Weitchie and turned to Maude. "Yes, Doctor Kingsley, we have them stopped, for now. Until the case can be presented at our court date late next month. I am sure they will not dare do any more work now." His eyes turned back to Weitchie like steel to a magnet.

Michael squeezed her slender waist as he sat beside and a little below her on a root. "That's good to hear. See darling, I told you it would all work out. It just takes a little time."

She looked at him for a moment, then back to Maude. "But all is not made right for long time?"

"Not yet, but soon. Attorney Jones can testify that you really do live here and that should settle the matter. Is that not correct, Mr. Jones?"

"Uh, yes, Doctor, I have seen her and can testify that she, well...lives here. It is stretching things a bit, and I never would have believed you if you had just told me this. Do you mind if I touch your ears? Not sure I trust my eyes right now." Weitchie shook her head, then nodded, leaning forward.

As the lawyer got up, Jeb laughed. "Hit all us menfolk that way, Lawyer Jones. None of us ever saw anything like this gal before, but stick around for a little and have some of this coffee. You'll believe."

The lawyer touched Weitchie's ears, both of them, and her hair, then stood back. "Amazing. I don't know what to think. No legal precedent I have ever heard of for this." He shook his head, looking a little dazed.

Maude nodded. "That is, of course, why I wanted you to see her. I am sure there is no precedent, but I understand the law has some flexibility to cover unusual circumstances. Is that not correct?"

"Yes, of course, but I'll have to think about this. Wouldn't do to take her into court." He chuckled hollowly. "The judge that will hear our case is fairly broad-minded, but...besides the inconvenience...you said she can't leave this grove?"

"No. Not at least until we plant more trees on her land."

"I see. Well, if we have enough witnesses that it would be a hardship for her to appear...she can sign papers at least. Should work out okay. No, thank you. No coffee. Ulcer. I must return to the city anyway. I truly am sorry we couldn't get here sooner, Miss Weitchie, but we will protect your rights, believe me. I will be in touch. Good day, everyone." So help me he actually bowed to Weitchie, then to Maude, before he turned and left with long strides. Maybe he was always in a hurry.

"Well, looks like we got things better now. More coffee? Anyone? Looks like we'll need another pot. Here come the others."

As some were getting refills the tall young environmentalist, never did get his name, and the two women came into the clearing. After greetings, Maude asked the tall fellow about the people who had been arrested.

"A few bruises and scratches, nothing serious. They are all out on bail, the ones that were actually booked. Most were just turned loose as soon as they were in town. Might get some fines when it all comes up in court, but that will be a while and we have a fund set up for that eventuality."

"And how you human think now for protection of my trees?"

The red-head answered. "It looks good, Weitchie.

Damned reporters didn't show up yesterday like they were supposed to, but they're interviewing everybody, so it should be in the papers if the publisher doesn't kill it. We got the word out to a lot of people and many will be on our side. The best chance the loggers had was before anyone knew the trees were here."

"What is 'reporters'?"

"I'll explain later, darling."

The other woman spoke up. "That's why we came to see you. The more publicity the better and the fall equinox is this Saturday. We try to hold some sort of environmental celebration at each solstice and equinox. If we could do one here in this grove, that would really bring a lot more people to our cause and give us more publicity. Keep the issue in the papers. Anybody that saw this grove would want to protect it."

The tall fellow nodded. "What do you folks think? Could we do that?"

Everyone turned to look at Maude, then Weitchie. Maude hesitated. "How many people would you expect to be involved?"

"Difficult to say, not a lot of people around here like to celebrate what the Christians consider pagan holidays. Perhaps a hundred, that's the most that we've had in the summer. Usually less in the fall and winter. It would be enough to make a difference in protecting the grove though."

Maude thought a moment, twisting one braid. "I suppose publicity is always useful in such a matter. There is a certain measure of safety in numbers when dealing with any governmental or judicial agency. Would you mind very much, Weitchie? Would you feel all right about meeting some people, letting them see you and enjoy your grove?"

"Some human not happy with me, and my animal cousins not like too many, but if you think those who come love my trees like you, and you say is good, Maude, is okay for me. If not too many then is okay."

They discussed plans for the celebration as I sat there watching her, and as they talked they got more enthusiastic and optimistic. I guess the morning's troubles faded from their minds pretty fast. Frank and the red-haired woman were quiet though. I didn't have much to say and I just listened, watching Weitchie as she watched the others. She didn't understand a lot of their talk, but she looked a lot better by the time I left. I caught a ride with some of the others as the sun went down in a brilliant, red-gold California sunset.

❦

Called in sick on Wednesday and didn't see Buck until the following Friday, which was September 22nd. As we drove home from another job, he asked me what had happened Tuesday afternoon.

"Come on, fella, you can tell ol' Buck, did you make out that night? Did you get that little red-head you were telling me about?"

"No Buck. Just listened while the folks there talked. Left at dark."

He sighed. "Ah well. All those hippies and weirdo protesters were there too, eh?" I nodded. "What're they planning next? Going do some more protesting? Better not mess with my cat again. No way. Next time heads get busted sure. Don't like 'em messing with my Melinda. No way."

"Don't think the ones I heard talking damaged the other tractor. They didn't say anything like that. They mostly just talked about legal stuff and having a celebration of some sort tomorrow, so more people would know about the grove. I think they're right, really should save this one, make it a park or something. It's different."

"'Cause you're hot after that chickee hangs out in

there? Hell, once the trees are gone she'll straighten out. Give you a better chance. Better for you if she was in town."

"It really is different there, Buck. Not like other groves we've worked. I wish I knew how I could help them save it."

"Come on, Joe-boy, I'm telling you, don't get so hung up on a few logs." Buck shook his head as he finished his coffee. "Just more lumber waiting for the saws."

"No, Buck, this one is real different. I can't explain, but it is."

"Got to get a bigger Thermos." Buck turned in the seat, looking at me, shaking his head as he put it down on the floor. "Not right for a hardhat working in the woods to carry books in his lunch pail. One way or another, it'll mess you up sure. 'Specially reading that fantasy stuff. For kids! Crazy for a working man, stuff like that. I looked at one of them books one time, like what you were telling me about in that grove over yonder. Birds, butterflies, and trees talking? C'mon! You're still thinking this little redhead is something different? Tell you, they're all the same. Where'd you get that kind of notion anyways? Crazy." He tipped his hardhat back, scratching his neck as we slowed for another string of motor homes that were trying to pass each other. Never did know why so many of them come north in the fall.

"Hey! I just remembered you telling me something about fairies and nature spirits and stuff once before—when was it—oh yeah, two years ago when we were helping to log redwoods down by Whitethorn. What in hell was the name of that place you were reading about? Find home? Something like that. That where you got these crazy ideas, Joe-boy? Where was that place?"

"Northern Scotland. Met a girl near where we were working had been to Findhorn, got me started reading some of their books. She was pretty strange, really believed in hugging trees and talking with them and things like that. Guess she was trying to convert me or something."

"Ha! More like she wanted to lay you, I bet. She a vegetarian, all that stuff? Pretty? Long hair and free love? You make out? Better'n reading!"

"No, Buck. Not like that. We just talked a couple of times, nothing more. I've lots of time evenings for reading, better than a couch potato tanking Coors before the tube. You'll ruin your insides and your brain."

He laughed, slapping his leg. "Knew I'd make it some day, Joe-boy." He took his hardhat off, looking at me out of the sides of his eyes. "Finally got a rise out of ol' Joe. Got a bet with Al, he never thought I'd do it."

"Doesn't have anything to do with this redwood grove where we were working. The woman there is really different. Not a regular human woman. Like her grove, she's different, and special."

"You got it bad, Joe-boy, never saw a worse case. Either somebody's pulling your leg or you're flipping out from all that reading and no beer or nooky." Buck picked up his Thermos and shook it, then laid it back on the floor and turned on his seat, facing me.

"Serious like, Joe, why don't you get yourself an old lady and settle down? Good for a quiet sort like you. You musta read that in one of your magazines—married men live longer. Saw a special on TV that said so. Be better for you, buy some property, settle down. Some good buys near here. This area's gonna grow." Buck chuckled and turned back to look through the windshield. "You have to admit it's pretty country."

"Yes."

"Yeah. And loggers gotta relax, Joe. Live a little." He turned to look out the window as we pulled into the shop yard. "Bet you ol' Barron's out for the weekend living it up, getting drunk and laid. Rich man like that, bound to be. Hear he's got a mistress and a party pad in the city. Bet you two weeks pay he's not letting a few trees spoil his fun."

"We'll see, Buck."

As I parked the truck in its space and got out, there were only a few fluffy clouds in the sky. It looked like the weather would stay fine for the celebration next day.

INTERLUDE: An angry Barron sits up straight behind his broad steel desk, one hand flat on the top, the other clicking a pen against his teeth. He drops the pen and picks up the phone. "Mabel, get me that damned attorney of ours again. Yeah, Josh Able....

"You heard what that damned judge did, Josh?...

"Right. What are you doing about it?...

"C'mon, Josh, you've got to do better than that. Put everybody on it. Hire more people if you have to, but get the search done....

"Right. Whatever it takes. I tell you I have to have those logs. It's make or break time. Now. You hear me?...

"Listen to me, Josh. If you can't find some heirs, or someone can pass, then think of something different. There has to be some way to break that injunction and that's what I pay you for....

"So....

"Josh. You've been getting commissions from me for how long? You want to continue on the gravy train?...

"I'm telling you! It is that serious. Yes. Brother-in-law, whatever, I want those logs....

"Yes, I'm going to call Attos, the CDF, the judge, everybody I can think of that owes me a favor. Every damned one. Yeah, the publisher too. He quashed that last rabble-rousing story in his paper, so I know we can count on him....

"Right, I'm calling in all favors on this one. You hear me? All!...

"That's better. I'll give you one more week....

"You're hearing me right. One more week....

"Good. I expect to hear from you in a few days. Bye, Josh."

Barron touches the button and dials again, sitting straight and staring at nothing through the big picture window.

8

FALL RAIN

...Next day I still wasn't feeling good, not sleeping very well either. Couldn't get it all straight in my mind. Felt like the time when I was a boy and climbed near the top of a tall tree. The branch I was standing on slowly bent, then suddenly broke right off. Felt like that now, as if the ground were about to fall out from under me. When I was a kid I could cling to the trunk and slide down, but this time it didn't feel like there was anything to hold on to, nothing solid. Felt like that as I went by to see Weitchie's grove on Saturday. It was beautiful out there.

Music, singing and dancing, food and games, kids running around in the bright sunshine, it was quite a gathering, their equinox celebration. The grove was always full of life and color since she woke from her sleep, birds, butterflies, and flowers blooming among the great trees. The people seemed happy, carefree, too, though there was not a lot of them. I counted two dozen adults, but with their kids it was enough to fill the narrow canyon.

Maude had bought Weitchie some new clothes and she looked beautiful, smiling for everyone and laughing with the children, but I felt she wasn't completely at ease. Maybe feeling a little tense, like she was not at all used to a lot of humans or real sure everything was settled about her trees. And I guess a lot of the adults thought she was in costume or something and didn't believe her. The kids didn't care if she was real or not; she was real enough for them.

I went by in the mid-afternoon but didn't stay long, just a few hours. Didn't feel comfortable with so many people either, mostly all strangers and for me it was noisy. Guess that's what the Bible means though, when it says, "Make a joyful noise unto the Lord". They were joyful, but I didn't feel like that. Maybe some of us are just too serious minded, or maybe too much inclined to see the dark side of things. Seemed to me they were trampling the flowers.

Weitchie's friends were all happy and optimistic. Even Frank was playing with the kids and dancing. Michael's cut was healing and he came over where I was sitting by his yellow tent and talked with me for a while, told me how it had been when he first found the grove and met Weitchie. Don't know why he wanted to tell me all about it, but I guess he was still jealous and just wanted somebody that wouldn't say anything back, just listen. Said he'd tried to talk to Maude, but she was a counselor who was used to giving advice and not much into listening.

When I left, Frank rode into town with me and we had a couple of beers together. That's when he told me some about himself, how he'd been arrested and put in jail the previous spring doing environmental stuff in Oregon. I kind of liked Frank; he had a lot of interesting things to say.

Everything stayed about the same for the next week. The weather was real fine with the beginning of Fall. It's often like that along the coast, the nicest time of year. Weitchie's grove was peaceful and quiet whenever I went by to watch her and listen to the others talk. It really looked like everything would be all right. Maude even placed an order for a thousand seedling trees from a grower. Gave them a down payment and was looking for people to do the planting after the start of the winter rains.

On Monday, October 2nd, at noon, Maude and Jeb returned from a court hearing and found a Sheriff's car blocking the old logging road. As Jeb pulled off the highway, two deputies got out of the patrol car and one walked over to the driver's side of the van and leaned down, looking in....

"Sorry, folks. We've had some trouble in here the past couple of weeks so we had to close the road. Have orders to keep everyone out. Sorry."

Maude slipped out from her side and walked to the front of the van. As Jeb shut off the ignition, the deputy straightened and moved to face her. The other deputy came around their car as Jeb got out too.

"I don't believe we have met before, officer. I am Doctor Kingsley. I represent the owner of the property along this road." She gestured toward the dirt road beyond the patrol car. "We have just returned from a hearing at the courthouse and we are aware of the misunderstandings and difficulties of the past few weeks. We wish to return now to our camping site to see that all is well there. That is part of my responsibility to the owner."

"Sorry, Doctor Kingsley, we have no instructions for making exceptions. The road is closed to protect everyone."

"I can prove I am the owner's representative. If you will call your office, I am sure that can be easily verified. We have just come from the courthouse."

"Sorry, ma'am. No exceptions." The deputy straightened and stepped back. "I'd appreciate it if you folks would move along now. We don't want any incidents with folks parking illegally along the highway."

"But, we..."

"Might as well go back to town, Maude. This fellow's

got his mind full set on the matter. Won't likely change it with talk."

Maude stared at the two deputies for a long moment, then sighed. "We have our camping gear in there. There are things I need." The deputy stood adamant. Maude glanced at the deputy's badge then took a deep breath and turned toward the van, then went back to say, "We will return to the courthouse and ascertain the cause for this excess of zeal. Then we shall return here."

Later, that afternoon, Maude and Jeb found Frank waiting in the small organic cafe in Arcata where they had agreed to meet. As they walked in, he nodded to them soberly. "I heard. Told you it wasn't going to be so easy. Those bastards don't give up until you prove you're stronger and that you're gonna make them pay through the ass. Give them a real shitfit, that's all they understand. Power and money."

Maude turned toward another table, but Jeb sat down next to the shorter man, so she paused and finally pulled a chair out, sitting across the small table from him and dropping her heavy purse to the floor.

"You know the deputies are blocking the road into the grove?" Frank nodded and took his leather hat off, setting it on the floor. Maude continued, "We went by the sheriff's office and they said that blocking the road was the sheriff's orders and he could not be disturbed. They were hardly even civil." He nodded, she shook her head. "The court hearing this morning went as expected and Attorney Jones said everything was proceeding as it should, but now we can't reach him either. They say he is out of town. I definitely do not understand all of this. Something's amiss."

Jeb looked at her soberly. "Seems there's maybe more to it, Maude. More than shows on top."

"You're damned well right there's more to it. Those assholes are up to something and if we're going to save those trees we have to fight fire with fire. Set our own backfire. We'll never beat them on their own hypocritical, bullshit turf. We gotta fight our way and hit them where it hurts them most at least cost to us. The only way we'll ever get to these turkeys with their heads up their asses is by hitting their wallets. That's where their power lies—and their hearts, if they've got any. That's where they're vulnerable. The wallet. Just like the Boston tea party. Only things they know or care about are the dollar signs on the bottom line. Got to make the bastards pay for every inch of road, every stick of wood, every..."

"No. We will not engage in any further violence or destruction. Wrecking that tractor was more than enough. It was barbarous behavior."

"Ah shit, I didn't have anything to do with that, wasn't even there. Wish I had been. Anyway, can't you see it yet? I tell you these mother-rapists have the system rigged. You can never win playing their game in their casino. The cards are stacked, the dice are loaded, the wheels are magnetized. Why do you think that shit-fer-brains sheriff can't be disturbed, and your fancy pants lawyer is suddenly out of town? Why?"

"Attorney Jones is a reliable man. He comes very well recommended, and he has been forthright with us thus far. He warned that it would not be easy or done quickly, but he insisted just this morning that we certainly can win."

"Sure, you'll win someday. But what if they go in and cut the trees while he's playing out his lawyer's funny money game. The law may be on our side in the end, but don't you realize that the whole set-up is a big-assed game to the lawyers? The politicians who make the laws are mostly lawyers, the judges are lawyers, then we suckers go for advice to a lawyer. Their first loyalty is to the game. The law game. Sometimes that means justice, accidentally, sometimes not. Justice doesn't matter to them, just their sucking game and the money they make from all the poor damned fools like us."

"I have never met a more sarcastic, cynical, surly, and censorious person in my whole life, never such a mocking, miserable misanthrope. You sneer at everything around you. You..."

"Ah now, Maude. Easy. Let's get some coffee?" Jeb put a hand on her arm as he waved at the waitress. Frank sat still, eyes locked with Maude's. "Frank maybe gets a bit carried away, but he's got a point. It's a lawyer's game. Even I can see that. Likely it's best we try every way we can."

Maude took a deep breath and pushed her braids back over her shoulders, glancing at Jeb, then back to Frank. "You have some facts perhaps, but your interpretation is badly skewed. You distort everything to fit your distorted perceptions, though no more than might be expected with such a natal chart. You might at least try improving your life focus as well as cleaning up your language and your person. Try appreciating the good in the system and in people instead of condemning everything and everybody you see. Your perceptions are distorted and you..."

"I do appreciate. I really do," Frank said quietly, in his hoarse voice. He sighed and picked up his hat, then stood looking at her. "I appreciate the great trees, the wholesome earth, and all the beautiful wild things and places that're being destroyed." He jammed the hat on his head and walked to the cash register, reaching for his wallet.

Maude bit her lip, then stood. "Frank, wait." He turned. "Come back and sit down. Let us talk more about this." He did, after paying his bill.

She picked her heavy purse up, then set it down again. "Perhaps you are partly right and we need to deal with this situation in more than one mode, on more than one level."

Jeb straightened, setting his cup down. "You've hit it Maude, carrot and stick. We need 'em both. Try every way."

Frank looked at them both. "So? Don't think these brown brains know much about carrots, but you're right in this much: I don't object to what you are doing, playing the law game and all, all I ask is you leave me free to do my thing, my way. The more ways we hit them the better." He half grinned at Jeb. "The old police high-low is a better way of saying it. You talk to them nice and polite, play their legal games, and I'll shove their chainsaws up their ass. We'll see which does the job best. Sue them for all you can, and I will work to make them pay twice, three times over, for every inch they get. For every tree they destroy. That's the way. Keep after your lawyer, I'll keep after their balls. Which they carry in their wallet. Agreed? I support you in your method; you support me in mine. Or at least don't hassle me."

"Very well, but...oh hell. Do what you must."

"That I will."

Jeb smiled at both. "While we're sitting with our coffee, what about young Michael and our girl out there? They'll likely be wondering."

"Yes, we must get word to them. We haven't seen them since yesterday morning. Have you, Frank?

"No. Not since Saturday. Cops blocking the road, the damn loggers may be in there now for all we know. I was just going to walk in and check. Walk through the woods until I'm past that well-padded law wagon, if it's still there, then hike on in. May have to wait till dark, but moon's coming on to full in a couple of days. Almost too much light for nightwork."

"We will come with you. I have some things for Weitchie and Michael and you will need a ride out to the edge of the park."

"Okay, if you want to, but I don't let any moss grow on my feet."

"Reckon we can keep up all right, Frank."

That evening, they saw the deputies still parked at the turnoff to the old logging road, so they found one of the tourist redwood groves a little further along the highway and parked the van in the moon shadow. As she got out, Maude whispered, "What are you carrying in that pack, Frank?"

"What I always carry. Supplies. You don't need to know more. I'm camped in there, too, remember? No noise now." Maude looked at him, but he turned and led the way through the ferns banked along the highway.

They came into the grove just over an hour later. It's not really far from the highway, but it's slow going through the few groves left along the edge of the asphalt. Michael and Weitchie were waiting by her mother tree when Maude and Jeb arrived, followed in the dappled moonlight by a curious doe and her yearling fawn. As they caught their breath, Weitchie nuzzled the fawn, then turned to them.

"Is more of troubles, Maude? You come so late."

"I am not sure what is happening, Weitchie. We were in court this morning and it seemed that all was well, but when we returned at noon the road was blocked. We waited until dark and walked in."

Michael looked up from helping Jeb start a small fire. "How was it blocked, Maude? How do you mean? Who would block the road?"

"Two deputies in a patrol car, Michael. They would not let us pass. Has anyone been here? Have you heard any activity outside by our campsite?"

"No. Joe was by yesterday afternoon. Talked with us a little, then left. He's an odd one. Never has much to say, just likes to hang around watching. I would just as soon he didn't."

"Yes, he is shy and inhibited, but he is just a worker. In many ways a typical Virgo. Everything is all right here, then?"

"Sure."

"Yes, Doctor Maude. All well as may be with two more of my trees dying. All else is well."

"I am sorry, Weitchie, and I brought you some more clothes."

"Oh, thank you. I may now be like human female with many coverings? Is not so? You like me so, Mik-ail?" She laughed as she held up a blouse, then sobered. "But am troubled they block road. I feel they not have good feeling for me, my place, my trees. Not good feeling still. Your attorney and court give all human good feeling for my forest? They will love my trees when is all done? They not want to take more trees when court thing all finished?"

Michael put one arm around her as he sat beside her on the root. "We can't much help their feelings, darling. We can only stop them from their actions. Now that the court has agreed to hear our suit, we will win. We have justice on our side, and there's no more need for worry. I don't know why they blocked the road, but it's probably just some silly bureaucratic thing or maybe some sort of intimidation. Don't you agree, Maude?"

"Possibly, but I am not convinced that..."

"You got it right, Mike. Intimidation is a big part of their convoluted, white is black, big brother act. And they're good at it." Frank joined them, looking around. "The dumb asses even believe their own bullshit. Eat it for breakfast, lunch and dinner. Then feed it to the rest of the country. And the peasants lap it up." He sat on the log. "Really a great place here in this grove. If the bears don't eat you, it's a home."

"Frank, please restrain yourself, and find more civilized images for your conversation. What have you been up to?"

"I went by my tent, then I followed you in. What else?"

"Yes, what else? I can tell that you have been up to something."

Frank turned to Weitchie with a big grin. "You okay, foxy little red lady? You sure look good. All gods bear witness, if Michael hadn't got here first! Biggest mistake of my whole miserable life, walked all over the area and never saw this little canyon and the jewel hidden here. You sure you wouldn't like to dump this city slicker for a woods runner? Ain't I more your style now? This tall lady here will tell you I'm half an animal. You like animals, yes?"

Weitchie laughed at him, holding her hands out. "Man Frank, is sorry no more sister I have nearby. In past times have many sister dryad and good man always welcome." She looked down at the ground. "No more so now. Maybe sister in other redwoods by great water? Cannot tell with smelly place of machine between us, my trees gone."

"She means the highway."

"Yes. High-way. Bad place. My furry cousins not like it for bad smell, and many die there outside natural way. Very bad place. No trees can grow there. They want make high-way come here?"

"No, Weitchie darling, they will not pave the road into here. We will make a gate to stop all cars and trucks when we have won the suit. They would not pave a road to here anyway."

"Don't bet on it, Mike. Condominiums here someday if those bastards have their way. Unlimited growth! Pave the whole planet! Eradicate all wild things—and people! Make the world clean, neat and orderly for all unfeeling assholes!"

Maude stood, staring at Frank. "They will not have it their way here, and I would really appreciate it, Frank, if you could restrain yourself if you can not make a positive contribution to the discussion."

"I didn't say they *were* going to pave into here, and it'll damn sure be over my dead body if they try." Frank looked at Maude, shaking his head. "Those stumps out there, Maude, they're driving me nuts. Redwoods try to put up new growth from old burls. They don't die quick, you know? Can't you feel them, Maude? They're trying so hard to live!" The grove was quiet for a long moment. Frank was a feeling sort of fellow under all his rough talk. Often said things like that.

"Sorry I ran out of coffee ever'body."

"We really should return to town, Jeb. I promised to meet with those people at the North Coast Environmental Center tomorrow morning. And we had better not leave the car by the highway all night. Someone might tamper with it."

"Long lady, now you're beginning to get your butt into proper paranoia. And you're right. Knowing it's yours, they'll tow your van away if they see it."

"Are you coming with us?"

"Naw, thanks, I'll hang out here. If I go to that meeting tomorrow, you'll accuse me of grandstanding again. Being a rabble-rouser."

"I did not call you a rabble-rouser. I said you were a demagogue, one who arouses the emotions of his listeners through the use of inflammatory language. I think you really enjoy the concept and emotion of violence. You seek to encourage it at every possible opportunity."

"Well shit, I know what demagogue means and I damn well know what you meant. And I do. People need getting stirred up. Violence is good for the soul, so long as nobody gets hurt bad. But maybe that's hard for a female academic type to understand. It comes from below the neck; in fact, mostly from the crotch. You likely wouldn't know about that sort of thing."

Maude stood, clenched fists on her hips, staring at Frank.

"Please, friends, might there not be more of peace between you?"

Frank grinned. "Sorry, foxy babe. This hard-headed lady and me, we get kinda carried away, doesn't mean anything. We'll still work together and do what we have to."

"This person is right in that much, Weitchie: we will do all we can." Maude glared at the shorter man, lips compressed. "The Arranger of it all, for whatever reason She may have, has brought us together here and we will continue to work together until this matter is settled properly. Now we must depart and return to town. Please leave that tractor alone, Frank."

"Tractor? You mean that old yellow cat tractor out there? DC whatever? I'm allergic to cats, never go near them damn shit-eating things. Don't worry your long self, I'm going to bed. Busy day likely tomorrow. Night all." Frank grinned at Weitchie and left singing, the words of his song floating back through the bushes and the tall trees.

Oh flaccid prong, hope deferred
Of love's sweet bliss.
Emblem of limp despair, life's joys curtailed
Like hope, rising ever anew
To further neglect and sorrow
Of need unfilled, bachelor's woe....

He sang it again another time when I was there. Guess he made it up.

A few minutes later, Maude and Jeb made their well-wishes, and, following Frank, hiked back toward their car through the ravine, down the slope, and along the moonlit logging road.

By Wednesday morning the Sheriff's deputies were gone. I don't know why they blocked the road or why they left. Naturally they don't announce that sort of thing to the public, but guesses can be made. Maude had gotten back in contact with her lawyer and maybe he helped move the deputies. Seems he'd been called out of town by another client.

However it was, the weather finally broke after a dry summer. Not rain exactly, just a fine misty drizzle. Real nice after all the dust, but it did make things a bit slick. There was a thin layer of mud over everything where the coat of dust got wet. Most times a good strong rain will follow soon, and everything will be clean again, but that day, which was the next time I saw them, everything in the open had a thin coating of brown mud.

Weitchie's friends and some of the local activists were gathered at the entrance to her grove. They had piled the tree limbs and slashings out of the way, by the base of the tree that was leaning against the canyon wall, and were standing or sitting under another big tree that the drizzle hadn't wet yet. Guess they were having another conference. From what I saw of them, those folks liked to talk a whole lot. Never could understand that myself.

The brook that flowed out of the little canyon had been dammed up by the dirt and rock that Buck had pushed in for the skid road, but the water was beginning to back up and wash away some of the dirt, making a new cut for itself along one side of the ravine. Anyway, they were gathered under the first of the big redwood trees, nine of them besides Weitchie, talking there just past the two stumps and the pile of slashings.

Buck and I didn't know ahead of time what was about to happen. The boss just came by where we were working on another job and sent us out to the entrance to Weitchie's grove in the middle of the morning. We got there right behind the loggers. Maude told me later that she and Frank had been having another discussion just before we drove up.

"Some immature, infantile, and irresponsible person spray-painted graffiti slogans on that yellow tractor parked out there. Large '**EF!**s' and '**LUDDITES FOREVER**.' That is stupid, Frank."

"Good for the master-painter, keeps the soulless bastards nervous. Might make them think a little about what they're doing, butchering the earth."

"The Luddites were an absurd and ludicrous group who tried to stop industrial progress in weaving and cloth-making in England during the early 19th century. If they had their way we would still be wearing homespun or smelly animal skins. They would have stopped all progress. They wanted to..."

"Homespun and leather might not be so bad, they...hey! Shit! Look out! I thought I heard a truck, and here come the assholes again. Now it hits the fan! Everybody front and center!"

The ones that were sitting stood quickly and they all turned to look as six loggers walked up the ravine carrying their chainsaws, climbing gear, and other equipment. Buck had gone to his machine and was cussing under his breath, getting red in the face. His big yellow Caterpillar tractor had a lot of bright blue lettering all over it. I ran after the loggers and got there around the bend of the ravine right behind them. The other people had spread out, blocking the way. I looked, but didn't see Weitchie.

The first of the loggers stopped in front of Maude, setting his saw down. The others set their equipment on the ground here and there and stood watching. "You folks got no business being in here. I'll have to ask you to leave right now. We got work to do and it's dangerous. For your own safety, leave right sprightly."

Maude straightened, lips compressed. "You are very

mistaken. You are not going to cut any more trees here. This is private property, and we already have a suit against one logging company over the trees that were cut before. You are the ones that will leave, and immediately. We are getting very tired of this ridiculous business and our lawsuit can be..."

"Hold it, folks! Everyone stay right where you are!" Six officers came running up the ravine. The first, that same overweight Sheriff's deputy, was holding up his hand, stretching his over-full uniform. He puffed some as he came up behind and passed me, and I could smell his shaving lotion real strong over the smell of the damp earth and woods. Stopping, he took a deep breath.

"We've had some real bad misunderstandings around here in the past weeks and don't want any more of that. Now if you folks visiting here will follow me back out, and get in your cars and leave, there's no need for trouble. No need at all. We will all just walk down the way here...." As he spoke, the deputy turned, pointing back down the ravine. "What the hell are you doing here?"

The one the deputy yelled at was a skinny tall fellow with a TV camera on his shoulder, the little red light already on. The fellow stopped, one foot braced against the bank. Raising the eyepiece to his eye, he started sweeping the area while a small dark-haired woman right behind him was talking softly into a microphone, a recorder hung over her shoulder.

The deputy got pretty bent out of shape at seeing the TV people. He sort of swelled up and turned red. I was a bit worried for him. "Now look, there is no news story here. These folks just been camping nearby and visiting here and they're about to leave. I'll thank you TV folks to lead the way out. Right now, if you please." The two ignored the deputy and continued what they were doing, the cameraman panning the scene and the woman talking away into the mike, one eye on the fellow with the TV camera. The cameraman almost lost his balance when he tried to show the tops of the tall trees. Slipping, he put one foot in the brook but didn't stop filming for an instant.

Maude and the tall young environmentalist fellow stepped forward together toward the camera. The cameraman quickly focused on them while the small woman stepped forward, adjusting the recorder and holding the mike out. Maude got started first. "This Deputy Sheriff is badly mistaken. We represent the owner of this land and we have no intention of leaving, or of allowing any cutting of trees or other destructive work here on this private property."

The others gathered behind Maude, voicing loud agreement and I was starting to feel funny again, dizzy and kinda faint, having trouble breathing.

The tall, young environmental fellow took another step forward, and holding up a hand, he spoke in a loud voice in a forceful way. Guess he had talked to TV people before. "Sergeant Fowler just arrived here, and it seems that his office has again been misinformed about the situation here in this grove. As Doctor Kingsley has pointed out, someone in the timber industry has the mistaken idea that these trees are for sale. They are not. They have not been, will not be. That is final. We..."

"Now hold it there, damn you." The first logger shouted him down in a rough voice. "You're right there's some mistake. Nobody owns this land until the court decides on it. Meantime we have permission from the heirs of the original homesteader to cut these trees. You folks gotta leave right now, for your own good, or the deputies will take you out. Make up your mind right quick 'cause we have work to do and we're tired of this nonsense." He knelt by his saw, checking the oil and getting it ready.

The deputy, his ham hands on his hips, looked around at everybody like he was undecided what to do with the TV camera whirring away by the side of the muddy, rocky skid road we were mostly all standing on by then. Guess he had to decide one way or the other. "This timber worker is entirely correct. They have the proper papers and legal permission to take these trees. We are here to support their rights and to protect the public. It would be very dangerous for untrained persons to be around while they are falling and removing these trees. I must ask you to leave peaceably. Right now. If you do not, I will have to enforce the law and begin making arrests. Please leave peaceably, right now." The other five deputies closed up behind him.

A hoarse voice called out. "No way, asshole."

It was suddenly very quiet. Quiet enough to hear water drops falling off the trees and a bird calling back in the grove.

Buck had come up beside me and now he started forward, pushing through the deputies, heading straight for Frank who was standing back and to one side. "There you are, you little hippie bastard. Spray paint your goddamned shit on my Betsy will you? I'll..." Buck put his head down and charged. I started toward him as soon as I saw him move, but someone, guess it was a deputy, tripped me and I went face down in the mud, hardhat rolling away.

Everything went crazy. Buck grappled with Frank, then backed to swing at him. Jeb tried to help Frank, but a logger ran up and put a fist in his face. The redheaded environmental woman charged the logger, and then everybody was shouting and wrestling, slipping in the mud and tripping over the logging equipment. I got up and tried to get to Buck again, but somebody hit me from behind. I think he used one of the logger's tools that were laying there, so it must have been one of them. Don't know why he hit me, or why the deputies weren't moving faster. As I fell, I noticed the cameraman and his helper still recording, standing off by the end of the road in a clump of flowering rhododendrons and ferns, filming everything. Don't know how they got there. When I tried to get up again, somebody kicked me in the side of the head. Still got a scar there under my hair.

I never did get the rest of what happened sorted out for sure. When I talked to Maude and Jeb later, they were pretty confused themselves. Maude remembered everything else real good, but maybe she didn't want to remember that fight.

❦

When I came to, I was lying on a clump of grass beside the muddy, half-filled-in brook, right next to the big yellow cat with the bright blue lettering all over it. When I first opened my eyes it seemed like those letters were moving and squiggling about, and it made me even more dizzy. I rolled away and saw Buck sitting on a rock nearby, wiping brown mud off his yellow hardhat. He grinned when he saw my eyes open. I managed to sit up very slowly. "Hey, Joe-boy. Thought maybe I was gonna have to carry you in to the hospital to cat-scan that head of yours." He chuckled. "Or whatever it is they do to find out if anything's in there. If you can get up, guess I won't ever know." He started to laugh but stopped with a groan, holding his ribs. "How come you always end up laying around like this, Joe-boy? On company time, too. Every time we find a little bit of fun you're laying around. How come, Joe?"

Hearing the chainsaws echoing down the ravine and branches crashing to the ground, I got to my feet and turned to look back toward the canyon. Tried taking a step that way, but fell to one knee and nearly passed out again. Buck got up, putting his hat back on. "Now hang on, Joe-boy, the loggers are nearly finished for today. Just topping out and limbing a couple of the trees before they pack up for home. That little brawl kept them from cutting much this time. Let's get you and me into town and into dry clothes, eh? You look like something dragged out of a swamp by a alligator. Guess I'm not much better. Lousy spot for a little action. Don't look like you're bleeding anymore."

I turned to look at him, feeling stupid. "Where'd everybody go?"

"C'mon, I'll give you a hand over to the pickup. Already got your hat and tools." He put an arm around under my arms and started half carrying me toward the truck. I pulled back.

"Buck, wait. I got to..."

"Easy does it, fella. Nothing more to be done today. Like I say, the loggers are just finishing." I pulled away from him, turning back toward the ravine, but one of the loggers came into view carrying his saw on his shoulder and other equipment in his hand. Another followed him. They looked kind of funny at me but didn't say anything. I turned and walked to our light green truck, climbing in on the driver's side.

Buck followed. "Sure you want to drive, Joe?"

"Yeah, Buck. It's what I get paid for. Just give me a minute and I'll be all right. My head hurts some. Think somebody kicked me after I was tripped." I lay back against the headrest for a few minutes and touched the dried blood on the side of my head. Buck finished cleaning his hardhat and got in. I winced when he slammed the door, then sat up and started the motor, backing around, wheels slipping in the mud as I maneuvered past the loggers' trucks.

"What happened to everybody, Buck? Tell me."

"Sure, Joe, just take it easy, okay?"

"Yeah, Buck. Just tell me."

"Like I said, the loggers're just finishing up. Nobody much hurt, not your friends or that lousy dirty ape of a hippie who painted my Dolores." He snorted. "I laid a good one on him once, but he gave me a real tussle. Hell, it was a good match. I'm heavier, but he sure knows a lot of tricks. If a deputy hadn't gotten into it to help me, I might've had my hands full. Tough little bastard. Looked like he got some good licks in on the deputy, too, before it was over." Buck laughed, rubbing his chin, leaning over. "That deputy won't forget him real soon and I got me some sore ribs. Real tough fer a hairy little ape of a hippie."

"What did they do, Buck, the deputies?"

"Ah well, bunch of spoil-sports, you know how they are. Don't like to mix it up unless it's all on their side. Usually is. Hell, Joe-boy, they arrested 'em all. Cuffed every damn one and hauled 'em away. That's what they did."

"They arrested Maude and Jeb? And Frank? God, he was on parole. What about Michael? He didn't fight them. Buck, for God's sake tell me all of it."

"Well, sure, fella, just take it easy. Okay? I'm not sure what all your friends' names are, but the dark fellow I was fighting with, the tall older fellow was with the tall woman, the woman herself, and—oh yeah, Michael must be the fellow we saw couple of weeks back. With the big pack. Yeah, they took him. Not much of a fighter. Guess he was trying to stop the action, but he got it, too. Took all of 'em. Them environmentalists, everybody. Cuffed 'em and hauled 'em away. You know how the cops are? Just doing their thing. Real slick operators." He laughed again, then groaned. "Yeah. Mud slick. Hah! Have a hard time getting their pretty uniforms clean again, all that brown mud. Ow, my ribs!"

"But Weitchie, the small red-haired woman I told you about. The one who lived there in the grove. What about her? She couldn't leave. She...God!"

"Your sweetie? I'm still thinking you've been smoking

some funny weed there, Joe-boy. I never saw anyone like that. You think I wouldn't notice a pretty young chickee like that?" He turned on the seat, watching me. "Two women with that tall environmental fellow, one had red hair. Real feisty. Scratched a couple of deputies real good. Took two of the boys to get cuffs on that one!" He laughed again. "Ow! Spitfire for sure. There was two young fellows I remember from the last time they protested. Dragged them away, too. Hah. That going limp don't work so good in the mud." Buck took a last swallow from his big Thermos, still chuckling and holding his side.

"That's all. Took 'em all away. No little redhead. That couple from the TV went on their own way, after arguing with the deputy was in charge. He sure was pissed that they knew to come out here and film it all. Somebody at the sheriff's office must have tipped them. Guess the sergeant didn't figure he and his boys looked so good wrestling with those women." He bent over laughing again. "Ow, damn! That redhead sure going to embarrass those deputies, took two of 'em to cuff her. Had some of her clothes torn, too. All on film. God, got to quit laughing 'fore it kills me."

"Maude didn't fight, did she? The tall older woman?'

"Fight? Man you missed a good show. She musta had ten pounds in that purse of hers, Lord only knows what all. When two of the cops grabbed her old man she went crazy-like. Started swinging that purse like a baseball bat. Both hands. Yeah, man! They finally cuffed her, too. All of 'em cuffed. Dragged 'em out to the wagon. You say she was some sort of doctor or something?"

"From the university."

"Oh, that kind of doctor. Put up a good scrap. Whole thing reminded me of when we used to have tug of wars in a mud puddle in high school. They was near all of them head to toe mud." He chuckled again. "Ain't had so much fun in years." He turned in the seat again, looking at me.

"Don't take it so hard there, fella. Everything works out. Whatever will be, will be." I just shook my head. "They'll all get out on bail, if they're ever actually locked up. Your friend will make out all right. They're a tough bunch. I know." He rubbed his ribs with a groan.

"You don't understand, Buck, I know they'll be all right. It's the trees in the grove. They'll cut them all now. That's wrong. They shouldn't do that. Not right at all."

"Ah, come on, Joe. I know that bunch of trees is something special for you. You always been a dreamer, a idealist. I've known that for years. And I know you got a thing going there, but you got to face it. No trees got a chance unless they're protected by the government. Even the big trees that outfit down in 'Frisco raised money to buy, they had to put them in a state or national park to protect them. Worth a lot of money, those trees. A whole lot. Make fine lumber. Lots of people want that lumber."

"They're worth a lot more standing, Buck. You don't know how much more."

"Yeah, well, maybe those folks can do something. Heard they had a hot shot lawyer working for them. That's what it takes. Being only a single grove, not a lot of trees or a whole forest, maybe they can save them. Not our worry. Let's just get on home, Joe-boy, get a beer or three, get some grub, a hot shower and clean clothes." Buck scraped some drying mud off his knees.

"Really shoulda come with me last night, Joe. Won't hurt you to stop for a beer or two with the boys. Bet you two to one you'll feel better." Buck turned in the narrow pickup seat to look at me, grinning. I just shook my head. "Ah well. Can't get a rise outa you today. I tell you, Joe, let ol' BM worry about those trees and logs. That's his business."

As we approached the slick wet black asphalt of the highway, I slowed to stop before turning toward town and two buzzards rose heavily from beside the dirt road.

Guess they were feeding on more roadkill. We see a lot of that around here. A lot of stuff gets killed.

❦

INTERLUDE: Barron sits relaxed at his broad steel desk and leans back in his swivel chair, one arm over his head, grinning as he talks on the phone.

"Right, Josh, it all worked out. You did a damned good job and I won't forget it. No sir, I won't. You can count on it....

"Right. Those trees will keep the mill going for a few more days. Give me time to work out everything. Finances, relationships, the wife and Shirley, you know, all of that....

"You got it. It pays to have friends owe you a favor or two. Politicians need a lot of help getting elected. It costs big bucks, a lot of money these days. They need all the help they can get, and the smart ones don't forget who helped them when it counts....

"Right. That's the way of it. But these logs will only keep my mill going for a while, so I want your help in finding out if there may be some more of the old trees that were overlooked....

"Sure, it's not likely, but we missed this grove so there may be others. I don't have to tell you how valuable they are....

"Right. And one other thing. That TV footage and recording those people made by that grove. You took care of that?...

"Good. Knew I could count on you and old Budget down at the paper. Wouldn't want that kind of sensationalist material to get out. Might upset some of the workers and other people....

"Right. You understand, Josh. Got to keep the workers content, and all the folks out there happy. That way everything goes smooth and the politicians don't get a lot of hassle and the union's got nothing to complain about. But I'll tell you, I am sure glad this all worked out. It's a good thing I'd built up some favors or I could have lost those trees. Things are getting tougher every year in the timber business, but you have to admit the challenges are there....

"You could do with a few less challenges? Come on, Josh, where's your balls? Where's your manhood?...

"Ladies are enough challenge for you, eh? I can understand that, but politics and business are also great incentives. They keep the juices flowing—and the money....

"Right. Well, got to run. Thanks again, Josh. I won't forget your help. Bye, Josh."

Barron yawns, switches off the office computer and stands, stretching. He walks over to the picture window and looks out at the rain and wind-swept smoke, smiling as he pulls up his tie and shrugs into his blue blazer. He reaches for a raincoat as he turns off the office lights.

POSTLUDE

...Never lost anything that was important to me before that I know of. For the next four weeks I was numb, barely went through the motions at work or off. Took some sick leave, and when I was at work I wasn't really there. Hardly remember anything of those weeks, and it wasn't until Tuesday, October 31, Halloween, that I worked with Buck again. I remember that day because I was helping him pull the last of the big logs out of the canyon so they could load them on the logging trucks and haul them off to the mill. Don't know why they hadn't been taken out sooner, might have been the rain. It can rain real hard here on the coast once it gets started. Often does with winter coming.

That narrow canyon was a real mess with bushes, flowers, and ferns mostly broken down or crushed beneath loggers' boots or the heavy treads of the tractor. Mud everywhere, churned up, slashings pushed into piles out of the way, and the huge stumps. Hellish. Good thing it was still raining slowly, drops tapping on my hardhat, because not all the water running from my chin came from the sky. Don't know how I got through that day. Just numb and going through the motions like I'd done too many times before.

After we finished loading Buck's cat on the low-boy

trailer, I went back one more time to pick up a pigtail of cable, and, as I left, I paused in the ravine and stood there in the soft mud and looked back. Just stood there with the tears running down my face with the rain, looking back toward the ravaged grove. Yeah, I don't remember the last time I cried, sure not since I was a real young child. Wasn't much use to it then or now.

Buck pushed the button of the airhorn, its raucous sound blasting through the soft sounds of the rain. He was answered by a crow flapping across the mouth of the ravine. *Grawk, gawk, grraawk, gawk!* Guess crows don't much care as long as there is enough food for them, and there always is....

Without knowing exactly why, I raised my right fist above my head for a moment, then turned and walked to the truck, wiping my face with a bandana. Always carried a bandana in the winter, on account of the rain.

Buck didn't have much to say at first, but as we neared the highway he poured the last of the coffee out of his big Thermos into the plastic cup and started talking. "Sure makes a mess, logging, but it'll all grow back 'fore you know it. Those rhodies are tough, and the ferns and other bushes, they'll all come back soon enough. Probably go in and plant a lot of Doug fir seedlings, and first thing you know it'll all be a lively forest again."

"Yes, Buck."

"Won't hardly be any different." He took a last swallow from the cup and turned in his seat, looking at me. "Likely they will argue about this in court for a while 'fore it's all settled."

"Yes."

"Shame. You know, those hippie friends of yours, they were all right folks. Really all right. Tough."

"Yes, Buck. They were."

"Kinda sorry they had to lose, but that's the way it

is. Winners and losers. Anyway, we got our jobs, that's winning."

Buck straightened in the seat and leaning forward, banged his fist on the dash. "Hey man, I never got to go to college like most of those damned highbrow environmentalists. Too stubborn and proud, wild and running around after excitement. Booze and women." He paused, staring at me. "No money for me to go to college anyway. But my sons are going. Both of them. You can bet your ass they are. I'm putting part of my pay away for it. Years ago I set up a trust account for them. Probably never mentioned that. Or them. But I'll tell you, Joe, no damn environmentalist's going to stop me. That's winning!"

"Yes, Buck. I understand." The big truck bucked as it rolled over a depression in the road, then jerked as the heavy-laden trailer bounced over the same soft spot.

"You okay, Joe?"

"Yes, Buck, I'm okay."

"It's over, Joe. Wonder where the boss will send us next? Always need more roads and that'll keep us working. Always will need more roads."

"We'll see, Buck."

We came to the end of the old logging road, thick mud now, and I slowly eased the truck to a stop at the highway. That big Caterpillar tractor's a heavy weight dragging behind you. Gotta be real careful when you drag something like that.

Black plumes of smoke from the twin stacks whipped around the cab in the gusting wind and thin rain as I revved the big motor and pulled slowly out onto the smooth, slick, shiny black asphalt, heading for town and the shop yard.

Got fired the next day. Went in to quit after payday on the first of the month, but the boss was ready for me, and had my severance paycheck already made out. Guess I wasn't very popular around there anymore. Just as well.

I had lots of unemployment coming and I needed time. Never did collect any unemployment checks before. It didn't seem right somehow. Now I think different about a lot of things.

I was sick with myself for the next couple of months, all through November and December, the holidays especially. Angry some days, other days I couldn't stop crying, and some days I couldn't even bring myself to get out of bed or fix a meal. Couldn't think, just slept all day. Other times I didn't sleep at all for several days, didn't want to, didn't like the dreams. Tried getting drunk once, but that didn't help. Never did any of that before, except maybe crying when I was a baby, and I don't remember much from then. Remembered a lot of other things in flashes and had crazy dreams when I did sleep. Sometimes my mother, father, or sisters I hadn't seen since my early teens were in those dreams. Other days I just wanted to tear things up. Does that make sense? Can a man be real deep angry, confused, guilty, sick, all at the same time?

I went to the public library where I used to hang out a lot, and read some books on psychology. Read about depression, which sort of fitted me, but the books didn't answer my questions about anything that mattered, or tell why it all happened. Couldn't find answers that felt right for me. One night real late, when I couldn't sleep any more, I started howling like a wolf. One psychology book said that would be good to do. The landlady kicked me out the next day.

Slept under the trees for a few days, got rained on and muddy, caught a bad cold. Guess I was sort of unraveled for a while, sure wasn't doing any good. Seems there are a lot of different ways of paying our dues in life's club. There's no free ride, in spite of how some people like to think. Not real life...never has been for free.

Finally, after a few days of being homeless, I started thinking a little and coughing real bad, so I went to the city and bought myself a small camouflage tent and some camping gear. Odd, I never thought about doing backpacking before, maybe because I was in the woods so much anyway, and the men I worked with never went anywhere without wheels. Never walked off the job if they could help it.

After living out of that little tent for a while in the rain, mud, and cold, I took the money I'd been saving over the years, not knowing what to do with it, and bought a new pickup with a nice camper. Regular main-stream sort, right out of Detroit, nothing conspicuous. Started traveling along the coast, down to Big Sur and up north to Puget Sound, all along the Pacific coast. Walked a lot of beaches that were mostly deserted in the winter. Felt good, right, walking along a windy beach and sitting on rocks, down low, watching waves pound and crash around me. I knew that was kind of dumb because you never know when a big wave might come in and trap you or wash you away. I knew better but didn't much care. Sometimes as I walked along a beach, I would disturb seagulls tearing at a dead fish or something that had washed up. They would flap into the air, screaming and circling over my head. Sometimes I would find some rocks to throw at them, but never hit one. Guess none of it was really their fault.

One place I think is called Jones Beach, maybe Baker, anyway it's right in San Francisco, almost under the Golden Gate Bridge, so close to the city I could hear a city bus go by just over a low hill, but most times, mornings, no one else was there. One morning, a couple of days after Christmas, I sat for hours on the rocks at the end of the beach, just above the water, watching a little piece of two by four about eight inches long. The waves hurled that piece of wood against the rocks, then carried it back and threw it against the rocks again almost out of sight in the foam and spray. Dashed it against those rocks again and again and again.

After a time, the piece of wood finally stopped, washed up on the nearby sand, and I came back to myself. Got up stiffly and drove some more. Never will forget that knotty, splintered piece of two by four. Like it had my name written on it.

While I started carefully working into my new "job" I spent a lot of time in the remaining redwoods, and one day at the end of January I met Jeb in the shower at the Jedediah Smith State Park campground by the Smith River just south of the Oregon border. He and Maude were camped there for a few days and he invited me to their campsite for coffee. Sitting around the fire, after telling some of my story about spending time on the coast, I asked Maude about what happened after they were arrested that day last fall.

She looked at me for a moment then took a sip from her mug and stared at the small fire. "We were held in jail through the remainder of the week and over the weekend, on one pretext or another, so it was not until the following Monday that we could arrange bail. Jeb and I. They kept everyone separate from each other so we did not know what had happened to the others. Nor would the deputies tell us anything. Once we were out, we had to find our van. They had towed it to a used car dealer's lot in town, and it was necessary to get money to pay the towing charge before they would give us the key. It was a very long day."

Jeb grinned wryly in memory. "Sure was a real long day, Joe. More coffee?" I shook my head.

"We were not able to drive back through the park to Weitchie's grove until Tuesday, and then we found a ditch cut across the road. The road was completely blocked."

I nodded. "Sometimes they don't want people going

into an area, they get a backhoe and ditch an old logging road like that. They can fill it again easy enough if they want to get in there themselves."

"Yes, I guess that is what they did, ditched the road just out of sight of the highway. It was raining pretty hard in October, but we had our raingear and decided to hike in anyway. As we came near where we had previously camped, we met Frank. He had been released that morning and had cut across through the open slopes. It was very muddy. We walked into the canyon with him, but none of us had much to say to each other." She paused. I knew what they had seen.

Jeb sighed and put his cup down. "Sure didn't have much to say, Joe. Gloomy day, rain and fog and all. Looked like it'd been raining steady, the way water was running in the gullies. Big rough logs, all cut up and laying there in the canyon ready for dragging out. Took me back to the war, which I'd rather not think on."

Maude laid a hand on his arm. "When we got into what had been Weitchie's grove, the trees had all been cut and some of the logs had been dragged out by the road. Others were still lying where they had fallen with only the huge stumps still standing upright. The canyon floor was littered with limbs and treetops and the trampled bushes and ferns, although some had been pushed into piles. Some rhododendron bushes still had a few fading pink flowers hanging from their broken branches. The birds, butterflies, animals, they were all gone."

"It was real bad, Joe, but guess you've seen that sort of thing."

"Saw that one too, Jeb, but there will never be another grove like that."

"I believe you are right in that, Joe. I am afraid we will not see another in our time, which is growing short. We have been searching, but I am increasingly certain there are no more of her kind left. In times like ours, when people worship such icons as automobiles, machinery, tall buildings, institutions, and other human-made things, they are no longer able to perceive anything sacred about a grove of trees, a stream, a mountain, or anything of nature. We have lost so much."

I nodded as she looked at me again for a long moment. "There's still a few of us, Maude."

She turned back to the fire. "Yes, a few. Michael was released on bail before we were and returned directly to the canyon. He was still camped there when we arrived. He still had his little yellow tent set up next to the stump of the mother tree, there in the mud. He was in a bad way, Joe, not very coherent, and he seemed not to recognize us at first. He kept interrupting me as I tried to talk to him, wanting to tell me about a dream he had. A dream of Weitchie, slowly fading away." She stopped again for a few minutes, staring at the small fire in the concrete firepit. Neither Jeb nor I had anything to say while we waited for her to continue.

Finally, she looked up at me. "You have been on the beaches, Joe. From what I could understand of what Michael said it was like when one marks something deeply in the sand of the beach while the tide is coming in. Each wave washes away a little more until the sand is all smooth again and the marks are gone. He described his dream like that. Intense waves of feeling and Weitchie fading away slowly, fading a little more with each wave of feeling until she was gone."

"Was Michael okay, when you left?"

"He wouldn't leave."

"But, he..."

"He left with us eventually, but we had to walk in through the mud and talk to him for several days before he started to come to himself. He was very much changed. As we drove him in to town, he was like a child staring at the buildings and everything as if he had never seen things like that before. But he was very calm, and he seemed much older when we finally left him at the lot where they had towed his sports car.

Jeb cleared his throat and nodded. "Lost a lot of weight, he did, Joe, and growing a beard, his hair long, ragged. He sure looked real different."

"Have you heard from him since then?"

"Oh, yes. We were concerned, of course, so we sought for him and found him just last week. He has a cabin in Marin county now, off by himself in some woods near the town of Mill Valley. He was doing some writing, but I think his heart was not in it. He seemed most interested in his wood carvings. He had made carvings of plants and birds and animals and was working on more. I think he was building his skill to carve her."

The fire hissed and popped as a sprinkling of drops fell into it from the tall trees overhead. Jeb reached out and stirred it, adding two small pieces of kindling, then he picked up the coffeepot. "I reckon Michael'll be all right, but not likely he'll ever see another woman again. Guess that's how it is with some artist types. Kind of, you might say, obsessed."

"Think I can understand how he feels, Jeb. What about Frank? Have you heard from him?"

Maude hesitated for a long while, staring at the flames. Then she got up and got a raincoat out of the van, put it on and sat down again. "We have not seen him since that day we returned to the grove, but we spoke with some of the people in Arcata who said the authorities had revoked his bail and re-arrested him. When we finally went to court, they took us in and tried us separately. We asked, but they would not let us see him or send a message. You know he was on probation all along?" I nodded. "Seems odd that things like that happen in this country, that people can be locked up and their friends not get to see or speak with them. We found out later that he was sentenced to three years. We have been working on permission to see him, and I am sure we soon will. We are working on his parole also."

"Sort of thought the two of you didn't get along so well."

"You are right, we did not, until the end." She stopped, straightened, shook herself and went on. "That day by the stump of the mother tree, I broke down, too. I was trying to help Michael and...I haven't cried since I was a little girl, and I..." She buried her face in her hands.

The fire crackled and popped. We heard a couple arguing about something in a nearby campsite, and Maude straightened herself, wiping her eyes and blowing her nose on a tissue from the pocket of her raincoat. "Now I cannot seem to stop, Joe, not for long."

Jeb put a long arm about her. "Good for you, Maude. Best thing that happened for you since we been together."

"I suppose so, Jeb, but it is embarrassing when it just bursts out. I cannot control it and...oh hell, it doesn't matter does it?"

"Got some catching up to do is all, sweetheart. Smooth out one of these days." Jeb grinned at me. "I keep telling her I did the same after the war."

"But I do want to tell you, Joe, about Frank. He cried that day in the grove. We held each other and Jeb held us both...and Michael."

"Yeah, Joe, that was something, fer sure. Half the water falling wasn't rain. Near got washed away down the canyon with it all."

"I understand."

"Frank helped me a great deal that day. He and Jeb. They cried, too, but did not lose themselves in it as I did." She half chuckled. "They did not come unglued in the rain. It makes such a big difference when people can cry together. It really helps so much."

I nodded again. "What was that word in that story? Oh yeah, Grok. Something like that. Sharing water."

"Yes, you do understand." She smiled at me. "It was just the way he said things that offended me so, and I did not really listen to him. At heart, he was right. Jeb and Frank were actually the sanest ones of all. In the end Frank was basically right about everything." She blew her nose again and looked up at me. "You have changed a lot too, Joe. "

Guess that's what Maude meant by sane. Sane people know how to cry when it's time for that. Maybe I'm sane now, but I'm not sure. Doesn't seem to matter much anymore. "I decided Frank was right too, Maude."

"Did you, Joe? Is that why you left your employment? Changed your life."

"Yes." Didn't want to tell them more of what I was doing. "Tough about Frank, I guess he would like to have done more all along, but he was real afraid of going to jail again. Easy to appreciate that. I wouldn't much like it either. I noticed he wasn't around whenever the deputies were. He'd disappear. Until that last time. Took a lot of courage, that day, and maybe a kind of desperation. He knew what was happening and what would happen to him."

"Yes, he knew. Imprisonment is very difficult for him, but we will see him soon and there will be some way we can help. They cannot keep us apart. Will you tell us what you are doing now, Joe?"

I hesitated. "Just driving around for now, camping in the woods sometimes, away from the roads. Still got some unemployment coming."

"I see." She looked at me for a long moment, then picked up a piece of kindling, staring at it. "I have been reading about Deep Ecology and Gaia, Joe. Now it bothers me even more that all of humanity's eggs and sperm are in one basket, so to speak. One biosphere traveling we know not where into we know not what perils." She laid the small piece of kindling gently on the fire.

"Perhaps in part because I personally have come to an age where I can no longer deny or ignore my own mortality or carry fertile eggs. Also, perhaps, I have come to an age of some wisdom and no longer react to events from my genitals and frustrations. Who can say? What I am sure of is that I am very troubled and angered by the situation I perceive in our society, here in the backwoods as well as in the cities and centers of power. It troubles me that our society may already be moribund. Perhaps it is time now for action, time to set aside the meditation rug and move on to action. A time for finding new icons, new symbolic tools—and symbolic acts." She looked up at me with a crooked smile on her thin lips. "Perhaps even such a mundane icon as a monkey wrench or a stone hammer?"

She turned back to the fire. "Every person driving an automobile or truck without necessity, or flying to Hawaii for vacation, or wasting any sort of wood, even a little piece of kindling, all of it, all the self-centered and irresponsible behavior of our citizenry troubles me now. Even throwing a piece of kindling on a fire we don't really need for our survival or physical comfort disturbs me." The light drizzle turned to a heavy rain as it does around the redwoods sometimes, falling in cupfuls from the great trees above us.

"To live up to the potential for becoming truly human, humane, we must become more fully conscious of the wildness in our own souls, that which within our essence resonates with untouched wilderness. As Frank said, we must reject the rapacious ways of our present society."

Jeb nodded. "You're 'specially right, Maude, for them that've lost their roots and drift like tumbleweed across an arid place, scattering seed. Hard telling what may grow from that sort of seed. Not likely what we'd like."

She nodded, pulling the hood of her raincoat up, tucking her braids in. "We have all changed quite a lot, Joe."

"More coffee, Joe?"

"Thanks no, Jeb, Maude. I better get going before I get soaked. It's good to see you both again. Likely we'll meet along the way if you're also traveling."

"Yes. We will meet again, Joe. In the meantime, please be very careful."

"I will, thanks. Good night."

"Good night, Joe."

As I drove on along the narrow highway through the black night, heading north to my next piece of work, the rain came down hard, splashing fiercely off the shiny asphalt of the narrow highway, slashing into the headlights.

❦

It was that same night, driving north with the wipers clicking furiously, that I decided to write all this down. Didn't know how to begin at first, but read some books at a library and just started. Ran into Maude and Jeb again, three weeks later, and they liked the idea. Maude started telling me everything she remembered and she has a real good memory, which I guess goes with being educated. I took a lot of notes, used a recorder part of the time, which helped, along with them encouraging me.

That's mostly the whole of the story. That's it, though maybe I should tell you about my new "job" before I finish. Still working roads, that's my thing, dharma or whatever they call it. Sometimes do other things, too, but mostly roads. Don't help with building roads anymore, my new job is wrecking them, or wrecking road-building equipment. I work at stopping the loggers and others who destroy the wild places, work at keeping them out. It's really pretty simple: they can't cut trees if they can't drive to them. Also, the roads themselves are often the worst part of the damage.

Working all these years around roads and heavy equipment has been real helpful. I know how to build roads, and I know how to destroy them; how to ruin equipment and how to find and pull up survey stakes or realign them; how to block roads in different ways so it costs them to open them up again. I do everything I can that will stop the big companies that make their profits from destroying forests and wild places.

There are a few others in my line of work. I sometimes see signs of them as I travel throughout the west in the U.S. and Canada, but I figure it's best working by myself. It would be nice to have some company; it gets lonely sometimes, and some things would be better done with another pair of hands or eyes, but I never was very sociable so I don't know anyone I could trust, someone who would be right for this line of work. And they might catch up with me someday, the servants of the rapists, so it's better that no one else is with me if that happens.

I expect the FBI or some other agency has been looking for me. I saw Buck one day as I was passing through that area, and another time I saw some of the others I used to work with. They told me some real sharp men had been around asking about me. They can't know for sure, not yet. I've been very careful. Takes time and patience and thinking everything through three, four times, but that I can do. Always been like that.

Sometimes I talk to campers and hikers I meet out in the wild places away from the paved roads. I figure some way to let them know what I'm doing without saying much, and the right ones catch on real quick. It always surprises me how many understand without asking a lot of questions. Some help. They provide me with steel spikes for ruining tires, and other tools, and sometimes money when my unemployment and savings get low. Sometimes they even thank me, though I don't know why. I don't know their names or addresses, nor do they mine; we just arrange it so they leave what I need in caches. Don't carry tools and things around more than necessary and what I do carry is well hidden in the double bottom of my camper. Always cautious, I never even gotten a traffic ticket or traveled outside the country, so they don't already have me in their computers as somebody to watch. That's why I gave a false name at the beginning of the story. In fact, all of the names in the story are false. I just made them up as I was traveling around, looking for suitable "work projects".

Work projects that will make them pay. And pay. And pay. No, not revenge, I'm just trying to stop them from destroying the few natural wild places that are left. Especially the virgin forests. Frank was right, the only way they will stop is when there's no more profit. I make staying in the earth-raping business very expensive. Sometimes, when I'm awaiting an opportunity to work on a project I have lined up, I try figuring how much I've cost them. The big timber companies and the companies looking for oil, the mills and cattle grazers, anybody who wants roads into the wild places. I figure it's over a million dollars already. Maybe one of these days they'll give up.

I haven't hurt anybody, any person I mean, in spite of what they say, just machines, and profits. Wouldn't be right to her memory to actually hurt anyone, and I'm a careful sort anyway, always have been. Maybe the only thing about me that hasn't changed. Skunk can't leave off his stripe or a crow grow white feathers. And I can't stop being a Virgo.

Also, I should mention, I've never burned a tractor or anything like that. I use less dangerous methods, but I watched one time when some men did burn a big tree-harvesting machine. They didn't see me, and I followed them when they left. They were loggers. Guess they didn't like a machine taking their jobs.

It's the following year as I write this, the evening of May 1, Mayday. A cool spring rain patters lightly on my two-man camouflage tent and the dead leaves and branches piled around it, and sometimes rain splashes off the huge stump in front of the tent, making a fine spray through the no-see-um screen. Looking out through the screen, I can see seven tiny, green redwood shoots cautiously poking up through the slashings and weeds beside the silted brook that flows, thick with mud, through the ravine just below the tent. I'm set up in a narrow canyon near where they're trying to build a new logging road. No point in saying where, it's just one of the places where I work now.

I'm finishing the story in my tent, writing on the back of used paper while waiting for dark. Got a typewriter that I taught myself to use in the camper, but I keep the truck parked away from the action so no one will suspect. Might get one of those portable computers some day, be a whole lot easier. Found someone who will take my writing, edit it, and get it published so others will know. People can read it while I go on with my work. And I tell anyone that asks that I'm a writer, traveling around getting material for a book on tree harvesting. I'm actually writing it, too, with over two hundred pages already finished.

The rain is letting up now, and soon it will be dark, time for "going to work". As I put my writing away, two crows call nearby, complaining to each other as they settle down for the night. *Cawk, craawk, crawk, Crwk?* Don't know what they have to complain about, roads and clear cutting don't hurt them. As I unzip the door of my little tent and climb out on my hands and knees, two deer, does heavy with young, start and bound away down the ravine. They don't mind all the clearcutting either, makes for more grass and plants they like.

I stand and stretch and think about the work ahead. The setting sun shines red-gold under the edge of the storm clouds, making the green seedlings sprouting beside the brook look like solid gold. Like they were carved out of living, solid, green gold. I'll bet Michael would like that. I'll have to tell him next time I see him. She's gone, but life is still here. We haven't lost it all yet.